"*Come, Lord Jesus* is a much needed respite during what's become the chaos of Christmas. If you're feeling empty, desperately wanting to see Christ in Christmas, pick up this refreshing book and beautifully prepare your heart for His advent." -Mary DeMuth, *Worth Living: How God's Wild Love for You Makes You Worthy*

"I have admired Kris Camealy's commitment to making space for busyness detoxification and doxological reflection for many years. In *Come, Lord Jesus*, she invites us to follow her into moments of quiet contemplation designed to help liberate us from the chaos of the modern holiday season. Inside, we find she has led us to Jesus. Every heart that longs to 'prepare him room,' can be grateful for Camealy and this graceful guide." –S. D. Smith, author of *The Green Ember Series*

"Advent is a season with more layers and depth to it than I often have time to sink my spiritual teeth into. But Kris Camealy's words echo just the right balance of spiritual richness and inviting softness to make me feel at home in the season, welcome to enter in and stay long. It is a much appreciated invitation." -Colleen Connell Mitchel, *Who Does he Say You Are?: Women Transformed By Christ In The Gospels*

"Perhaps one of the reasons we fill our Christmas

season (and our ordinary everydays) to capacity and beyond is because we don't much like to wait for what's next...even when what's coming is Christ himself. Kris Camealy's *Come, Lord Jesus* invites us to slow down, to resist the pull toward filling our Christmas to overflowing, and to open a quiet, unhurried space for Jesus to enter in. Give *yourself* a gift this Advent season, and let this beautiful book illuminate for you the unexpected blessings that are born in waiting." –**Michelle DeRusha**, author of *Katharina and Martin Luther: The Radical Marriage of a Runaway Nun and a Renegade Monk* (January 2017)

"At no time of year do we live by bread alone, but during Advent we crave particular nourishment. In this small book you will find rich and satisfying food for an Advent journey. Kris Camealy's reflections are lyrical and Scriptural. They are inspiring and instructive. This book is ideal fare for those weighty waiting days before the Feast." -**Christie Purifoy**, *Phd* and author of *Roots And Sky: A Journey Home In Four Seasons*

"A beautiful invitation to press into the weighty work of waiting. With tender prose and warm reflection, Kris Camealy welcomes us to experience and embrace the tension of God with us, even as we anticipate his arrival. Receive these rich and memorable devotional readings as a blessing over this holy season." –**Deidra Riggs**, author of *Every Little Thing: Making A World Of difference, Right Where You Are*

"Kris Camealy offers a true gift for the holiday season that weaves together a rich collection of scripture readings, prayers, and meditations that guide us to a place of quiet contemplation and mindfulness of God's love for us. For those who find that the holidays are a spiritually frantic, hurried time, this book serves as a gentle guide into the stability of scripture." –Ed Cyzewski, author of *The Contemplative Writer* and *A Christian Survival Guide*

"This is the book for all the restless hearts in this season of rush. It's for the ones who are tempted by the urgency, but who yearn for something else– something more holy. *Come, Lord Jesus* offers just that. This book is an invitation into the quiet, the wonder, and the mystery of Advent. I felt my breathing slow while turning the pages. With her words, Kris Camealy offers a sanctuary for us all –where we can simply be still and wait on our King. –Jennifer Dukes Lee, author of *The Happiness Dare*

"I'm not a girly devotional person. They usually feel fluffy like latte foam: pretty, but no taste or depth. In *Come, Lord Jesus*, Kris Camealy has given us a devotional for those of us who are right in the middle of the waiting. She does not shy away from hard truths and suffering — from the heft of longing — but she also paves a way to wait in hope. Pick up a copy of *Come, Lord Jesus* not just for Advent, but for the year. You'll find a kindred soul to sit with you as you wait for the promise of redemption and all things made new." –Ashley Hales, Ph.D., writer at aahales.com, pastor's wife

COME LORD JESUS

COME LORD JESUS

THE WEIGHT OF WAITING

KRIS CAMEALY

Columbus, OH

For Kurt, Luke, Sam, Abigail and Phoebe who love Christmas.

Contents

Foreword

Kimberlee Conway Ireton

As I read through *Come, Lord Jesus*, my first thought was that I wished it were more grounded in Kris's life. She tells great stories on her blog, and I wanted this to be more like that. But as I read on and reflected further, I realized that these meditations are intentionally un-storied. As with her Lenten devotional *Holey, Wholly, Holy*, she has chosen not to make herself the main character. Instead, she points away from herself to the God she so obviously loves. Kris's desire, always, is to glorify the One who is the heart of her life and her work—and to encourage us, her readers, to do the same. She longs for all of us to surrender wholly to the holy love of God and to the refining work that God longs to do in each of our lives.

It is Kris's commitment to refinement—what the older divines would have called sanctification— that I find so refreshing. She understands that sin is real, and that it separates us from God. She understands that God keeps wooing us, His wayward, broken children, and keeps offering to cleanse us from all unrighteousness through the blood of Our Lord Jesus Christ. And she understands both that we keep holding back and that the only way to refinement (or sanctification, or holiness) is through the refining fire of absolute surrender. We must let God have *everything*.

This scrap of anger that I'm clinging to—I give it to You, Lord. That corner of contempt for a certain politician (but he deserves it, Lord!)—all right, fine, I give that to You, too. The niggling doubt that You're not who You say You are—that goes on the fire as well, Lord. The fear that keeps me holding something back (just one egg in this other basket, please!)—I have to give that to You, too. And this gift that I hold so dear and prize so highly—even that is Yours, though it feels like death to surrender it.

Kris understands all of this—the desire to cling and the desire to surrender, and the fact that we sometimes (often?) desire both things simultaneously—and she writes to strengthen and increase our desire to surrender. She writes to encourage her readers to let it all go, to offer it all up, to give it to Jesus as a sacrifice of praise. And she knows it's a sacrifice.

But the cry of her heart is always, *Come, Lord Jesus!* It's a cry echoed in every prayer in this book. She wants Jesus to be Lord everywhere—Lord of her heart, Lord of yours, and mine, Lord of this earth. She longs for His kingdom to come fully.

The saints of the Celtic tradition of Christianity often spoke of "thin places" where God's presence was more palpable, where the veil between heaven and earth grew thin and wispy and one could see and feel and sense the presence of God more fully than in other places. Advent is one of the "thin places" of the year. It is a time when we prepare for the coming of Christ. We remember and celebrate His incarnation, the thinnest of all places ever—Very God in human flesh! And we also look forward and celebrate His promised return, when the veil between earth and heaven will be forever parted and we will see the Kingdom of Heaven in all its fullness. Indeed, we will dwell there.

This is what Advent is—this two-fold gaze forward and back, celebrating and anticipating our Lord's coming—and this is what Kris longs to usher you into in this devotional. She joins her heartfelt cry of *Come, Lord Jesus* to the cry of God's people throughout the generations of the Church, and she invites you to raise up your voice in that prayer of petition, too:

Come, Lord Jesus.

Come into this world that is broken and beaten and weary and wounded and angry. Come shelter our poor, bruised, but still oh so beautiful planet beneath the shadow of Your healing wings.

Come in the stillness of night and the garish light of noon. Come in the mountains and on the shore and by the streams and in the cities. Come to my city, my town, my neighborhood, my house.

Come to me.

Come to my heart, my life. Walk inside. Look around with the holy love that is always in Your eyes. Do what You do when you come—turn everything upside down, turn me inside out so I can see myself clearly and run to You for shelter from my own ugliness and shame. Come lift my hanging head so I can see that You love me still. Come let me see myself reflected in Your gaze of love that makes me lovely.

Come, transform me, refine me, purify me in the fire of Your holy love. Come, fill my aching soul with Your love and gentleness and power. Come, let me live surrendered to You, surrounded by You, inspirited with You.

Come, let Your life flow through my veins.

Come, Lord Jesus.

As you read the words of Scripture and Kris's meditations on those words, as you read the prayers within these pages, my prayer for you in this Advent season is that the Lord Jesus would come to you, that He would meet you in these words and draw you to His Light, and that you would be filled to the measure with all the fullness of God, that Our Incarnate Lord would fill you with Himself. Amen. Come, Lord Jesus!

Introduction: The Weight Of Waiting

If the word *Advent* (from the Latin, *adventus*) means "coming" then for us it implies that we are waiting for something–or *Someone*. The notion that something, *Someone*, is coming, leads to the anticipation of the awaited arrival. Tension builds as we wait, and for many of us in the Western world, waiting is not something that comes easily to us. Our culture fosters and encourages impatience, with the never ending effort and money spent in attempt to make things happen faster. Faster food, faster banking, faster weight loss, faster downloading.

We are a people uncomfortable with and unaccustomed to waiting. Waiting requires a measure of discipline; it demands patience, and if we will lean into that space, waiting teaches us something of our own sanctification. A recent commercial I heard on the radio confirmed our culture's outright rejection of waiting, when a woman in a banking ad sort of sneered, "to me, impatience is a virtue." Many of us do not wait well.

Advent in the church, is a season of preparation rimmed with hopeful expectation. For 23 days before Christmas, we find ourselves waiting for Jesus to come. We busy ourselves with preparations–shopping, wrapping, baking, traveling, partying. Few of us manage to wait quietly. Instead, we fill our calendars with a steady stream of activity, perhaps in an attempt to distract ourselves from the stand-still feeling of the required waiting. Waiting is hard work for people who crave instant gratification. We want to see Jesus *now*.

> "The waiting is not just an indolent 'waiting around.' We wait 'for the morning,' which is to say that we wait in hope."
> [1]

We're not the first people who've lamented the seemingly slow gestation of the Holy. From the first exile out of the Garden of Eden people throughout the centuries have been waiting for their King to come. *Come, Lord Jesus* they have prayed and during Advent we find ourselves uttering the same three words. *O Come, O Come, Immanuel,* we sing, weary from the waiting. Immanuel, the name Isaiah gives us for the coming King (Isaiah 7:14), means *God with us*. He *has* come and *is* coming. One day, He will come *again*.

The Advent season provides us a beautiful, and sometimes difficult, opportunity to practice waiting. We won't do it perfectly. There will likely be more tasks, more invitations, and more opportunities for distraction on our calendars than we can manage. What if we took just the next few weeks to sit still just for a few moments, to let ourselves feel the weight of waiting? What if we slowed ourselves enough to whisper *Come, Lord Jesus* and then gave Him unhurried space to enter into us? How might the space and pace of waiting affect how we experience the unbridled joy of Christmas and the hope of Immanuel?

I'm attempting to lean into waiting seasons, to let God grow in me, a holy patience for the things promised but not yet revealed. I pray for us both, as we travel together this Advent season, that our hearts would be further opened to the Holy Spirit and that in the deliberate rejection of the hurried, harried, frenetic cadence of the Christmas season we would encounter Christ in our midst—*right here* among us even as we wait for Him.

> From of old no one has heard or perceived by the ear, no eye has seen a God besides you, who acts for those who wait for him. Isaiah 64:4

DECEMBER 1: WAIT

Today's Reading

Oh that you would rend the heavens and come down,
that the mountains might quake at your presence—
as when fire kindles brushwood
and the fire causes water to boil—
to make your name known to your adversaries,
and that the nations might tremble at your presence!
When you did awesome things that we did not look
for,
you came down, the mountains quaked at your
presence.

From of old no one has heard
or perceived by the ear,
no eye has seen a God besides you,
who acts for those who wait for him.
You meet him who joyfully works righteousness,
those who remember you in your ways.
Behold, you were angry, and we sinned;
in our sins we have been a long time, and shall we be
saved?
We have all become like one who is unclean,
and all our righteous deeds are like a polluted garment.
We all fade like a leaf,
and our iniquities, like the wind, take us away.
There is no one who calls upon your name,
who rouses himself to take hold of you;
for you have hidden your face from us,
and have made us melt in the hand of our iniquities.
But now, O Lord, you are our Father;
we are the clay, and you are our potter;
we are all the work of your hand.
Be not so terribly angry, O Lord,
and remember not iniquity forever.
Behold, please look, we are all your people.
Isaiah 64:1-9

Wait

Desiring God's tangible presence has been a long-lived

ache of the human heart since nearly the beginning of time. Where man once enjoyed daily physical fellowship with the Holy, sin cut a rift in the fabric of that friendship leaving a gaping hole in the hearts of mankind. A hole that can only be healed with the turning of hearts back towards the very One it once rejected.

"Oh, that you would rend the Heavens and come down," the people of Israel lament. Be present *with* us, they begged. It wasn't only God's presence they longed for, but to see the might of God on full display. "Rend the heavens," they plead. Tear open the veil and be here *with* us. Make the mountains shake, set fires, cause the whole earth to tremble. These are tremendous requests. Who would ask for such a display of power? Desert people. Hungry people. People who have finally come 'round to the confession and admission of their rebellion.

God has been working from the beginning, from the very first exile, on the hearts of His people. Tenderly, sometimes fiercely, God puts His finger into the hole left in the hearts of man, not to injure but to heal. But His healing hurts. We shrink back, turn around and like the ostrich, plunge our shame-filled heads into the quicksand of life. We live desert seasons, unwilling or unable to face the repentance God calls us to. We imagine that God is hiding from us, but it's we who have turned our hearts away and hidden our faces. It's we who have crossed our arms in defiance. When at last we awaken to our sin, when we see the ways it has manipulated our hearts, the cry comes from our lips–*come, Lord Jesus*.

In our awakening, we see that God has been doing "things we did not look for" all along (Isaiah 64:3). He has always been acting "for those who wait for Him." In our sins we have been a long time, and shall we be saved (Isaiah 64:4-5)?

In all our desert wandering we see God has not shut Himself up in the heavens out of reach of our cries. Salvation *is* coming–and has come. He has a plan. In our confession, we wait for it. In our admission of great need, God declares redemption. God would tear open the tapestry of Heaven to deliver unto us the very Prince of Heaven and lay Him low in the filth of our constant struggle.

We shall be saved.

A Question For Reflection In The Waiting
How am I wanting to see God move today?

God you have graciously called us out of our perpetual sin and made a way for us to see your might and power at work in our lives. Help us to pay attention. Uncross our arms, turn our chins toward you and heal us, by the perfect, indwelling presence of your Holy Spirit. Come, Lord Jesus, we pray.

2

DECEMBER 2: RESTORE US

Today's Reading

Give ear, O Shepherd of Israel,
you who lead Joseph like a flock.
You who are enthroned upon the cherubim, shine forth.
Before Ephraim and Benjamin and Manasseh,
stir up your might
and come to save us!
Restore us, O God;
let your face shine, that we may be saved!
O Lord God of hosts,
how long will you be angry with your people's prayers?

You have fed them with the bread of tears
and given them tears to drink in full measure.
You make us an object of contention for our neighbors,
and our enemies laugh among themselves.
Restore us, O God of hosts;
let your face shine, that we may be saved!
But let your hand be on the man of your right hand,
the son of man whom you have made strong for yourself!
Then we shall not turn back from you;
give us life, and we will call upon your name!
Restore us, O Lord God of hosts!
Let your face shine, that we may be saved!
Psalm 80:1-7, 17-19

Restore Us

It's not always easy to say *I'm sorry*. These words stick in our throats and on our lips. Sometimes, we have to wind our way around to getting them out like we're working our way straight through the knots of our transgressions in order to eventually untie our tongue to apologize. But when we do finally come around to apology, our heart hopes for ready acceptance. A genuine apology comes wrapped in a hunger for forgiveness. It's restoration we want, it's what we know we need.

Restore us, O God; let your face shine that we may be saved!
(Psalm 80:3).

Four times in this brief passage, the psalmist petitions God for salvation. "Save us!" He writes in repetitive desperation. "Restore us," he begs. "Hear us," the psalmist encourages. And our hearts cry out for the same. During the hustle of Advent our needs become vividly apparent. In our weariness of struggling to prepare our homes, and our hearts, we hunger to be heard, to be restored, to be saved.

Save us, restore us. These words spoken in contrition lead to healing and restoration. These are the foundational layers of repentance–the recognition that our salvation and restoration cannot come from within.

> When something breaks down or does not go as planned, we are given a glimpse of our great need, like a vast emptiness. We pray for solutions, crying out for immediate help, but God desires to give us more. To give something real. Something we can see with our eyes and feel with our skin. Like a baby born to us.[2]

I used to wonder about the repetition of certain scriptures, but now I understand it is not written as such for impact alone, but also for our comfort. We, too, like our ancient ancestors, are a people who forget. We live in different times are but plagued by the same hereditary heart condition of those who have gone before us. How desperately we still hunger for salvation. How lonely it can feel, waiting for the light of the Son to warm our faces.

A Question For Reflection In The Waiting
Where do I need to experience God's restoration today?

Merciful God, we call out to you—hear us, blessed Father! In our distractedness we have wandered. In our petulance we have tilted our chins away from you. We know that you are the only one who can save us from ourselves, from temptation, from the strife and striving of this world. Come, Lord Jesus, we continue to pray. Give ear to us. Restore us. Teach us what it means to live as a child of God.

3

DECEMBER 3: IN EVERY WAY ENRICHED

———

Today's Reading

Grace to you and peace from God our Father and the Lord Jesus Christ. I give thanks to my God always for you because of the grace of God that was given you in Christ Jesus, that in every way you were enriched in him in all speech and all knowledge—even as the testimony about Christ was confirmed among you—so that you are not lacking in any gift, as you wait for the revealing of our Lord Jesus Christ, who will sustain you to the end, guiltless in the day of our Lord Jesus Christ. God is

———

faithful, by whom you were called into the fellowship of his Son, Jesus Christ our Lord.

1 Corinthians 1:3-9

In Every Way, Enriched

When we were children, we used to spread ourselves and a stack of glossy catalogues across the family room floor beneath the twinkling lights of the tree. Armed with markers and scratch paper we'd circle, record, and dog-ear the shiny pages making note of everything we hoped to receive for Christmas. Before coming to know Christ, it was the tangible gifts we longed for the most in this season. As children, our longing was purely material, for in those days we didn't understand the season to be anything more than this. That gaping heart-hole still lingered and so we stuffed it full of plastic and cardboard dreams that never lasted long enough. We had not yet experienced the transformative touch of Jesus in our hearts.

> You are not lacking in any gift as you wait for the revealing of our Lord Jesus Christ, who will sustain you to the end. (1 Corinthians 1: 7)

Our culture still lures our hearts with man-made, mass produced enrichment. Paul reminds us here, as he reminded the people of Corinth, that because of the grace of Jesus we have what we need *in* Christ. The experience of knowing Jesus enriches our hearts and lives completely. In Him, we lack nothing. In this season of want, as we await His coming, we remember that our lives are rich with grace because of Christ, who did come, who lived among the people, who lives among us still. He makes His home in the hearts of those who love Him, however imperfectly we may live that out. We lack nothing because in Christ we have everything. His truth and glory revealed to us not only in Advent, but in the everyday moments of our lives, remind us that it is He who sustains us as we wait for His return.

The shiny temporary pleasures advertised to us this hungry season pale when propped beside the magnificent majesty of the King of heaven. He is our hope, our perpetual promise of righteousness to come, the fullness of heaven in human form, plunged low and raised again for our sake.

Rather than grab hold of the temporary to fill our need, we can and ought to recall the generosity of God who sent His own son that we might have fellowship with Him in the fullness of His glory. He is with us as we wait. He has come and will come again. What we ache for most this season can't be found between the pages of a magazine. The very gift we need most we already have! Advent invites us to recount the goodness of His grace–remember the gifts we have been given already, rest in the enrichment of Jesus, and anticipate what's more to come–*Adventus!*

He is coming.

A Question For Reflection In The Waiting
What do I need most from God today?

Jesus, your Word tell us that all we need is found in you. You are the living embodiment of our hope, our salvation, and the promise of eternal life. Turn our eyes this season from the temporary satisfaction we crave and plant in us a constant hunger for you alone. Remind us in the waiting that you have already enriched our lives in every way, providing us with every good gift that we don't even know we need. Come, Lord Jesus, help us to wait patiently for you.

4

DECEMBER 4: STAY AWAKE

Today's Reading

"But in those days, after that tribulation, the sun will be darkened, and the moon will not give its light, and the stars will be falling from heaven, and the powers in the heavens will be shaken. And then they will see the Son of Man coming in clouds with great power and glory. And then he will send out the angels and gather his elect from the four winds, from the ends of the earth to the ends of heaven.

"From the fig tree learn its lesson: as soon as its branch becomes tender and puts out its leaves, you know that

---

summer is near. So also, when you see these things taking place, you know that he is near, at the very gates. Truly, I say to you, this generation will not pass away until all these things take place. Heaven and earth will pass away, but my words will not pass away.

"But concerning that day or that hour, no one knows, not even the angels in heaven, nor the Son, but only the Father. Be on guard, keep awake. For you do not know when the time will come. It is like a man going on a journey, when he leaves home and puts his servants in charge, each with his work, and commands the doorkeeper to stay awake. Therefore stay awake—for you do not know when the master of the house will come, in the evening, or at midnight, or when the rooster crows, or in the morning—lest he come suddenly and find you asleep. And what I say to you I say to all: Stay awake."

Mark 13:24-37

Stay Awake

Advent comes with an unbearable weight, the expectation of Christ coming. We hear the echo of these words from 1 Samuel: "Who is able to stand before the LORD, this holy God?" (1 Samuel 6:20). While we ache for Him, we struggle to remain in His presence. The world and all of its shiny temptations distracts us. In our weariness we relax our watchful gaze. Today's passage from Mark reminds us that Jesus' return is sure. We will see signs of Jesus' return. Warnings, clues, a pre-recorded series of events we can trace through the book of Revelation. Yet, His coming will surprise us. We will not know the day or the hour.

"Be on guard, keep awake." These are Jesus' own words to us. Pay attention, He encourages. Advent comes every year at a pre-determined time, marked on virtually every calendar available. We know exactly when it will begin. We know when it will end. We see the signs of Advent's impending arrival in the stores, and on TV in advertisements. But Christ's urgency to his disciples reminds us that we don't really know what we think we know. He is coming, but we do not know when. Christ warns us to wait–awake–lest He come suddenly and finds us asleep.

We have work to do. The season of Advent offers an opportunity to prepare not only our homes for the Christmas season, but our hearts for the second Advent. We must remain awake, faithful and focused, even when the temptation to hibernate presses in. Wakefulness requires a conscious effort to be present, even in our distraction and weariness. Advent invites us to hold on. We cannot afford to sleep through our lives.

Stay awake, He urges. Pay attention. Be present. He is coming again.

A Question For Reflection In The Waiting
How can I be attentive today, to the voice of God in my life?

Jesus, you graciously and generously warn us about the danger of living with our eyes closed. So often we're caught sleep-walking through our lives. Helps us to see you in this season. Open our eyes and hearts to the work you have called us to, and teach us what it looks like to live alert, ready and faithful in the face of innumerable distractions and temptations to check out. Come, Lord Jesus, fix our eyes on you and strengthen us to stay awake.

5

DECEMBER 5: EVERY VALLEY LIFTED

Today's Reading

Comfort, comfort my people, says your God.
Speak tenderly to Jerusalem,
and cry to her
that her warfare is ended,
that her iniquity is pardoned,
that she has received from the Lord's hand
double for all her sins.
A voice cries:
"In the wilderness prepare the way of the Lord;

make straight in the desert a highway for our God.
Every valley shall be lifted up,
and every mountain and hill be made low;
the uneven ground shall become level,
and the rough places a plain.
And the glory of the Lord shall be revealed,
and all flesh shall see it together,
for the mouth of the Lord has spoken."
A voice says, "Cry!"
And I said, "What shall I cry?"
All flesh is grass,
and all its beauty is like the flower of the field.
The grass withers, the flower fades
when the breath of the Lord blows on it;
surely the people are grass.
The grass withers, the flower fades,
but the word of our God will stand forever.
Go on up to a high mountain,
O Zion, herald of good news;
lift up your voice with strength,
O Jerusalem, herald of good news;
lift it up, fear not;
say to the cities of Judah,
"Behold your God!"
Behold, the Lord God comes with might,
and his arm rules for him;
behold, his reward is with him,
and his recompense before him.

He will tend his flock like a shepherd;
he will gather the lambs in his arms;
he will carry them in his bosom,
and gently lead those that are with young.
Isaiah 40:1-11

Every Valley Lifted

Trace your fingertips across the surface of a topographical globe and you'll get a small sense of the earth's uneven terrain. The earth beneath our feet is anything but flat. For all of the mountain peaks and valleys we can see, climb and descend, there are innumerably more hidden beneath the vast oceans of the world. It is in this crooked place that we make our homes, where we are tried and tested by the humors of this uneven planet. The ripples of life leave us stumbling, exhausted, weary and defeated. But this is not how it will always be.

> Every valley shall be lifted up, and every mountain and hill be made low; the uneven ground shall become level, and the rough places a plain (Isaiah 40:4).

One day, God will grab hold of the edges of the earth and straighten forever the wrinkles that sin has gathered in its fists. Things now are not as they will be. Isaiah tells us that this leveling out will reveal the glory of God (Isaiah 40:5). The superficiality of the Christmas season, perpetuated by our culture, is like the grass that withers and blows away. The trees dry up, the wreaths lose their needles, the Christmas cookies are all eaten up, the candles burn down and the ornaments will be packed away. The things of this earth will fade, but in God's perfect, appointed season, He will mend what sin has broken. We will celebrate for eternity, a perpetual Christmas, in the very presence of Jesus.

The highs and lows of this life will one day be made straight by the merciful and just hand of our loving Father. The fragile, temporary of the world will slip from existence, like a vapor that burns off in the heat of the sun. What seems unjust will be rectified, what is torn will be mended. All brokenness will be replaced by permanent healing. He will gather us, His lambs to Himself, gently and mightily carrying us to the place where every valley is lifted and the uneven ground is level.

A Question For Reflection In The Waiting
What are the valley's in my life that cause me to stumble repeatedly?

God in heaven, how mighty is your love for us, your wandering lambs. Though we stumble through life valleys and struggle to stand on the mountain tops, you remind us that one day you will make all things straight. You promise us an unending Christmas celebration in Zion, where we will no longer wither and fade. Help us remember this. Teach us to look forward to living in your forever-presence. Come, Lord Jesus, be our hope this hour, and every moment until that time. Help us to wait.

6

DECEMBER 6: THE KISS OF RIGHTEOUSNESS AND PEACE

Today's Reading

Lord, you were favorable to your land;
  you restored the fortunes of Jacob.
You forgave the iniquity of your people;
  you covered all their sin.
Let me hear what God the Lord will speak,
for he will speak peace to his people, to his saints;
  but let them not turn back to folly.
Surely his salvation is near to those who fear him,
  that glory may dwell in our land.

Steadfast love and faithfulness meet;
righteousness and peace kiss each other.
Faithfulness springs up from the ground,
and righteousness looks down from the sky.
Yes, the Lord will give what is good,
and our land will yield its increase.
Righteousness will go before him
and make his footsteps a way.
Psalm 80:1-2, 8-13

The Kiss of Righteousness And Peace

Today's reading paints a magnificent picture of the covenant God has made with the earth and His children who inhabit it. The tenderness of this passage reveals the loving character of God who cares deeply for His creation, even in its brokenness.

> You restored the fortunes of Jacob.
> You forgave the iniquity of your people;
> You covered all their sin (Psalm 80:1-2).

Restoration, forgiveness, covering–these words fill our hearts with hope and gratefulness for what God has offered us through Jesus, the prince of heaven. He will speak peace to His people (85:8). These words unabashedly reveal God's tender mercy with images of love and faithfulness meeting, righteousness and peace kissing–what a vision this offers us! These words remind us that God's presence is life-giving, His faithfulness springs up from the ground (85:11). The covenant of Jesus promises fruitfulness and increase. With such a beautiful promise of God's goodness, it's a wonder that we would even be tempted to return to our folly, as this passage calls it, to our sin and foolish living. But we will and we do. Which is precisely why we need Immanuel in the manger and on the cross.

We can scarcely look on this passage with our eyes fully open. It's too magnificent a vision to behold. Can we even imagine what this kind of passionate love looks like played out? On the ground, this heavenly covenant looked like an expectant couple fleeing for their lives, a dirty stall, a humble manger, a baby King born in secret in the filth of a stable floor (Luke 2:1-20). This homeless Prince preaching a message of repentance and love, grace and mercy (Matthew 8:20), which lead to a mock-trial, torture, a cross (John 18:28-19:42) and finally, an earth-quaking, kingdom-shaking resurrection (Luke 24).

God's covenant of love looked nothing like this dreamy vision of *righteousness kissing peace* described here, and yet this is how God paints it for us–in broad strokes of redemptive red and cool hues of baptismal blue. God dapples the edges of this image with life-giving green and lights up the horizon with a hot yellow, the blazing light of heaven. This, a shining romance between God and His creation, a tender wooing of His wayward bride back to Himself, a brilliant depiction of the glory that will come. The painting that God has crafted here for us is in actuality, more than we can bear.

A Question For Reflection In The Waiting
In what areas of my life do I see evidence of God's passion-fueled covenant with me?

God of the Universe, you are so much more than we can bear. There is no way we can wrap our hearts around all that you are, and so instead of asking this of us, you come and dwell in us. When tuned to you, the overflow of our hearts mirrors tiny fragments of your glory reflected in the world around us. Your fingerprints are undeniably everywhere. Train our eyes to see you, and as the hymnodist writes, tune our hearts to sing your praise. Come, Lord Jesus, let us taste the sweetness of the kiss of righteousness and peace.

7

DECEMBER 7: KAIROS, NOT CHRONOS

Today's Reading

But do not overlook this one fact, beloved, that with the Lord one day is as a thousand years, and a thousand years as one day. The Lord is not slow to fulfill his promise as some count slowness, but is patient toward you, not wishing that any should perish, but that all should reach repentance. But the day of the Lord will come like a thief, and then the heavens will pass away with a roar, and the heavenly bodies will be burned up and dissolved, and the earth and the works that are done on it will be exposed.

Since all these things are thus to be dissolved, what sort
of people ought you to be in lives of holiness and
godliness, waiting for and hastening the coming of the
day of God, because of which the heavens will be set on
fire and dissolved, and the heavenly bodies will melt as
they burn! But according to his promise we are waiting
for new heavens and a new earth in which righteousness
dwells.

Therefore, beloved, since you are waiting for these, be
diligent to be found by him without spot or blemish, and
at peace. And count the patience of our Lord as salvation.

2 Peter 3:8-15a

Kairos, Not Chronos

God is not bound by the man-made calendar by which
we all use to manage our lives. Of course, knowing this
doesn't prevent us from growing anxious as we wait for
prayers to be answered, circumstances to change, new
seasons to come, or hard seasons to end. In Greek, there
are two words for "time", *kairos* and *chronos*. *Kairos* means
"opportunity" or "fitting time." This time is not
quantitative or measurable by anything concrete, but is
rather like a season. The span of kairos cannot be cupped
in our hands or nailed down with a calendar appointment.

Madeline L'Engle described *kairos* as, "that time which
breaks through with a shock of joy, that time we do not
recognize while we are experiencing it, but only

afterwards, because it has nothing to do with chronological time."[3] It is essentially, *God's timing*.

Chronos, on the other hand, is the time we most relate to. This is what we set our watches to and mark our dates by, a measurable, chronological version of keeping track of life's events, moments and hours. Consequently, this is the version of time we tend to prefer. Chronos is the version of time we often assume when we pray, and wait for God to act. But today's reading reminds us that with God, a day is like a thousand years, and a thousand years, one day (2 Peter 3:8).

In other words, God isn't operating in *chronos*, but rather acts according to what He determines to be the "fitting time," *kairos*. How discouraging this can seem to us as we wait! What we're tempted to miss in the waiting is what we cannot see–what God is working behind the scenes for our behalf. When we imagine God to be slow, or even late, it is because we have assumed, even expected, (dare I say insisted) that God operate according to the timeframe that suits *our* comfort. We want to force Him into *chronos* because we can track that. We perpetually forget that God's ways are not our ways.

> For my thoughts are not your thoughts, neither are your
> ways my ways, declares the Lord. For as the heavens are
> higher than the earth, so are my ways higher than your
> ways and my thoughts than your thoughts (Isaiah 55:8-9).

Peter reminds us here that we are waiting for a new heaven

and a new earth where righteousness dwells. These moments and seasons of our lives are all leading up to this one final time when the things of the earth will no longer be as they are. Advent turns our gaze to heaven, as we await Jesus' coming again. Like the shepherds in the field, we too look to the sky for signs of His coming. And we wait. Keeping in mind the mystery of God's impeccable timing makes the waiting more bearable while encouraging us to hope.

Count the patience of our Lord as salvation (2 Peter 3: 15a).

The time God gives us in the waiting is a gift, whether or not it feels that way in the moment. He is not late in His coming. The Lord is not slow to fulfill his promise as some count slowness, but is patient toward you, not wishing that any should perish, but that all should reach repentance (2 Peter 3: 9).

A Question For Reflection In The Waiting
What am I waiting for right now?

Lord, how good and generous you are to give us each day of our lives. Help us to remember that every hour is a gift, and teach us to use the minutes wisely, to learn the way of repentance, to wait patiently for the new heaven where righteousness dwells. It is hard to wait for you, God. Be with us as we struggle. Teach us what it means to live according to kairos. Come, Lord Jesus, we pray.

8

DECEMBER 8: PREPARE THE WAY

Today's Reading

The beginning of the gospel of Jesus Christ, the Son of
God.
As it is written in Isaiah the prophet,
"Behold, I send my messenger before your face,
who will prepare your way,
the voice of one crying in the wilderness:
'Prepare the way of the Lord,
make his paths straight,'"
John appeared, baptizing in the wilderness and

---

proclaiming a baptism of repentance for the forgiveness of sins. And all the country of Judea and all Jerusalem were going out to him and were being baptized by him in the river Jordan, confessing their sins. Now John was clothed with camel's hair and wore a leather belt around his waist and ate locusts and wild honey. And he preached, saying, "After me comes he who is mightier than I, the strap of whose sandals I am not worthy to stoop down and untie. I have baptized you with water, but he will baptize you with the Holy Spirit."

Mark 1:1-8

Prepare The Way

In today's reading, Mark recalls for us the words of Old Testament prophet Isaiah. He prophesied about the mission of John, Jesus' cousin, born to Zechariah,(a priest) and his (barren) wife Elizabeth. The scriptural accounts of John sketch for us the image of a curious man, flocked in camel hair and leather, a man who ate enough honey and locusts for it to be noted as his food source, a man seemingly more comfortable outside the city gates than inside, a man who people puzzled over even as they were drawn to him. Neither John's odd appearance, interesting dietary choices or message of repentance and salvation isolated him. The nearby townspeople flocked to him.

And all of the country of Judea and Jerusalem were going

out to him and being baptized by him in the river Jordan (
Mark 1: 5).

A missionary by training and calling, John spent his life
on the move fulfilling the prophetic call of his own life,
in order to prophesy about the coming of Jesus. John was
born for this very purpose (Luke 1:13-17). Our own lives
too bear the mark of calling. God continues to call us first,
to repentance then to mission. While the culture shouts
the material beauty of the Christmas season–lights,
ornaments, parties and gifts; our lives might offer a less
flashy, but far more exciting narrative–sin, repentance,
grace, manger, cross, resurrection! When we tell the true
story of Christmas, even to our own hearts, we make room
for Jesus to come fully in. We cannot tell the story without
remembering our own need for a Savior. There is someone
among us who needs to hear a truer version of the story,
the version that tells it like it was, like it is still, and how
it will be in the end. This is the story where you *want* to
reveal all of the spoilers. John proclaimed a baptism of
repentance for the forgiveness of sins (Mark 1:4), his voice
calling out into the wilderness, the barren, Christ-less
places of the world and prepared the soil of hurting hearts,
a place for Jesus to enter in–to fully come. His words are
for us today, even as they were for the people of Judea
and Jerusalem. In order to prepare the way, we must make
a way for our own hearts to receive Him by way of

repentance. John calls us to our knees, to the edge of the water to be washed.

> We must prepare the way. We must prepare God's path to our hearts, to cultivate an awareness of how near the Holy One bides, how immediately he accompanies every moment, how beautifully and sweetly he attends our every breath.[4]

We turn from our sin towards the face of Jesus where we can learn a new way of living. Not that we won't still stumble, not that we won't still forget and fumble and wrestle, but that now we have His constant company in the places of doubt, discouragement and dissent. This truth transforms our hearts. It means that now, we carry the greatest story of all time everywhere, sealed on our hearts. Our own redemption in light of His. How can we keep this to ourselves? Who do we know that needs to hear that this season is about so much more than twinkling lights and fresh cut trees and magical tales of gifts tucked secretly beneath them? Maybe it is us. How easy is it to lose sight of the richness of the greatest Gift in the noise and clutter of the mad rush to Christmas. How distractible we are. Because of the Holy Spirit, Jesus is already *with* us. Won't you tell this story? Again and again, tell it.

A Question For Reflection In The Waiting

———

What extra burden am I carrying this season?

Jesus, how humble you came, without the pomp and circumstance that makes us giddy, but lowly in a manger, in the meek form of a fragile baby. You slipped into a world blanketed in sin and struggle and longing, and made your home here for a time, calling all to repentance and salvation, filling us with your Holy Spirit to help us to live unashamed, as John did. Teach us to tell your story to others, that they too might find salvation and that your Holy Spirit might dwell in the hearts of all who hear your truth. Come, Lord Jesus, bring us to repentance, that we might know you intimately in every season.

9

DECEMBER 9: GOOD NEWS

Today's Reading

The Spirit of the Lord God is upon me,
because the Lord has anointed me
to bring good news to the poor;
he has sent me to bind up the brokenhearted,
to proclaim liberty to the captives,
and the opening of the prison to those who are bound;
to proclaim the year of the Lord's favor,
and the day of vengeance of our God;
to comfort all who mourn;
to grant to those who mourn in Zion—

---

to give them a beautiful headdress instead of ashes,
the oil of gladness instead of mourning,
the garment of praise instead of a faint spirit;
that they may be called oaks of righteousness,
the planting of the Lord, that he may be glorified.
They shall build up the ancient ruins;
they shall raise up the former devastations;
they shall repair the ruined cities,
the devastations of many generations.
For I the Lord love justice;
I hate robbery and wrong;
I will faithfully give them their recompense,
and I will make an everlasting covenant with them.
Their offspring shall be known among the nations,
and their descendants in the midst of the peoples;
all who see them shall acknowledge them,
that they are an offspring the Lord has blessed.
I will greatly rejoice in the Lord;
my soul shall exult in my God,
for he has clothed me with the garments of salvation;
he has covered me with the robe of righteousness,
as a bridegroom decks himself like a priest with a
beautiful headdress,
and as a bride adorns herself with her jewels.
For as the earth brings forth its sprouts,
and as a garden causes what is sown in it to sprout up,
so the Lord God will cause righteousness and praise
to sprout up before all the nations.

COME LORD JESUS

Isaiah 61: 1-4, 8-11

Good News

After three Spanish journalists were freed from captivity in Syria in 2014, a Spanish newspaper's website called their release a *miracle*.[5] Their release *was* miraculous, given the climate of the region in which they were taken and held for six months. While the captured journalists knew without question that they were indeed, prisoners, many of us would not use the term "captive" to describe ourselves. And yet here, Isaiah uses that very word to describe God's people.

For many of us, captivity doesn't look like a jail cell or a prison camp in a closed country. Rather, the captivity holding so many of us hostage looks more like remaining trapped in our brokenness, living out the daily struggle against our pet sins, stumbling around, buried beneath grief, battling an attitude of ingratitude or living enslaved to the habitual nursing of our broken hearts. Despite our financial standing, many of us live desperately poor in spirit, suffering from spiritual malnutrition, masked by the affluence of our churches, our communities and our friendships. We are a people who have so much, and yet many of us live in our (not so) former devastations.

Good news stories like this one about the Spanish journalists give us hope for other captives. They remind us of the possibility of miracles. And today, right now,

Isaiah offers us another *good news* story, the one of our *own* release.

> He has sent me to bind up the brokenhearted, to proclaim liberty to the captives, and the opening of the prison to those who are bound; (Isaiah 61:1).

Here, Isaiah reminds us, as he did the people of Israel, a people who knew true captivity, that God has not forgotten His beloved. This hopeful passage speaks a message of good news to our hearts. God loves justice–not the kind we tend to think of, but heavenly justice. The kind of justice that turns earthly kingdoms to rubble and raises the lowliest to the highest. God's justice included springing open prison doors, caring for orphans and widows, turning lowly shepherds into kings who lead great nations, and restoring enslaved people to the land from which they had been exiled. God's justice included the sending of Jesus, His own son, to absorb the punishment for all sin, for all time. This is the good news. The *best* news.

As we await this Advent for the fulfillment of God's ultimate recompense, let us live no longer as captives in our sin and brokenness, but as prisoners of hope (Zachariah 9:12). Let these promising words of Isaiah bind our wounds and relieve our grief. Let this hopeful passage drip like sweet oil over you, removing the ashes that have once been your uniform. Though we wait, we claim the joy of the Lord with our shouts of thanksgiving and praise for this, the good news!

A Question For Reflection In The Waiting

In what ways am I living as a captive right now?

Gracious God, how generously you have extended your love and mercy on us, a people often more comfortable with captivity than in the realm of your holy freedom. You transform our mourning into dancing, and bind our broken hearts to your own, grafting us into your family through the sacrificed body of your own Son. Come, Lord Jesus, help us to identify not with the captivity of the flesh but to instead celebrate that we are in your custody as prisoners of hope. Let this truth sustain us as we await your coming.

10

DECEMBER 10: FROM GENERATION TO GENERATION

Today's Reading

And Mary said,
"My soul magnifies the Lord,
and my spirit rejoices in God my Savior,
for he has looked on the humble estate of his servant.
For behold, from now on all generations will call me
blessed;
for he who is mighty has done great things for me,
and holy is his name.

And his mercy is for those who fear him
from generation to generation.
He has shown strength with his arm;
he has scattered the proud in the thoughts of their hearts;
he has brought down the mighty from their thrones
and exalted those of humble estate;
he has filled the hungry with good things,
and the rich he has sent away empty.
He has helped his servant Israel,
in remembrance of his mercy,
as he spoke to our fathers,
to Abraham and to his offspring forever."
Luke 1:46b-55

From Generation To Generation

From now on, generations will call me blessed. Perhaps there is none more so than Mary, who can recount for us the faithfulness of God. Chosen above all women to carry the holy seed of heaven in her womb, to nurture and grow in the secret place, the very body of the God-baby who would be King, the Prince of heaven unfolding in her belly. For all accounts Mary was no one of any stature or position. She lacked the credentials one might inspect with scrutiny when choosing a surrogate to carry a Savior. And yet, God did choose her, and she would bear the Son of the Almighty, who would choose *us* at the high cost of the cross.

In Advent, we find ourselves steeped in a season of

desire and want. For many of us, this includes taking the time to select and purchase gifts for those whom we love, specific things we know others desire. Perhaps we too have shared our own list with a loved one. But more than the material, deeper than the want of something useful or decorative, somewhere in our hearts, resides the desire to be chosen by God for something special, something amazing. Many of us long for something that only God can give–we are, each of us, waiting for some kind of miracle. For some of us, perhaps this desire is nearer to the surface than it is for others. But before you reject this thought, consider for a moment the long awaited, yet unfulfilled longings of your heart. What would it mean to see that hunger born into the world, satisfied by the Holy hand of heaven, delivered unto you, as a gift, free and perfectly? How might that impact your view of God? Or the rest of your life?

...he has filled the hungry with good things (Luke 1:53).

The blessing of Mary, through the gestation and delivery of Jesus, remains one of the most controversial miracles ever recorded. Never before, and never since, has there ever been another virgin birth. Of all people from the beginning of time, God chose this one young woman, and no one else, for the birth that would change the entire world forever. And here, in this passage, Mary recognizes the magnitude of what God has done and she worships.

She calls out the good faithfulness of God, reciting the mighty movement of His actions throughout history. She tells us that for those who fear Him, His mercy will stand, from generation, to generation (Luke 1:50). In other words, God has already chosen and will continue to choose us, again and again. He chose us first in Eden, then in Egypt, the wilderness, in Israel, Gethsemane, and finally, on the cross. He chooses us now, in Advent and all of the church seasons that come in between and after.

Through Mary, God chose us, all these generations later. Out of her obedience and willingness, the miracle we long for has already come to us. Jesus. *Immanuel.* We are already filled with the only thing that can meet our every need. As A.W. Tozer said, "The man who has God for his treasure has all things in One. Many ordinary treasures may be denied him, or if he is allowed to have them, the enjoyment of them will be so tempered that they will never be necessary to his happiness."[6]

A Question For Reflection In The Waiting
In what ways can I see how God has chosen me?

Merciful God, holy and perfect One, you blessed us

through Mary with Jesus. You chose a humble woman to be the mother of your Son, and by choosing her, you remind us that we too, are chosen. You are all that we need, your goodness, mercy and love are the fulfillment of all of our longings. Come, Lord Jesus, show us what it means to live as Mary did, humble, willing, eager to serve and honor you in all things. Continue to shape us in the image of your perfect Son, in this and every season.

DECEMBER 11: LIKE THOSE WHO DREAM

Today's Reading

When the Lord restored the fortunes of Zion,
we were like those who dream.
Then our mouth was filled with laughter,
and our tongue with shouts of joy;
then they said among the nations,
"The Lord has done great things for them."
The Lord has done great things for us;
we are glad.
Restore our fortunes, O Lord,

---

like streams in the Negeb!
Those who sow in tears
shall reap with shouts of joy!
He who goes out weeping,
bearing the seed for sowing,
shall come home with shouts of joy,
bringing his sheaves with him.
Psalm 126

Like Those Who Dream

What does it feel like to dream–to slip into that fluid mind-space of imagination where good things seem possible, where hope runs like a river, sloshing up over the banks of our reality dousing every inch with unfettered possibility? If you've ever given yourself permission to imagine freely like this you know it as a joyous, spacious place for the soul to wander. Today's Psalm speaks about God's restoration of man with this kind of happy release.

> When the Lord restored the fortunes of Zion, we were like those who dream. Then our mouth was filled with laughter, and our tongue with shouts of joy (Psalm 126:1-2).

The Psalmist invites us into such a place, with gladness. Mouths filled with laughter, shouts of joy, gladness and a river flowing–signs of hope, life and restoration. What a vision! Waiting seasons can seem like a difficult time to cultivate a dream life. But maybe, it is the *perfect* season for it. The anticipation that builds during seemingly dormant seasons may be the invitation our hearts need to imagine, to dream of possibility. What if we don't receive it this way? Maybe for some of us, the waiting is instead a season of fear and hesitation, a paralyzed place of one-track thinking that blocks our heart's ability to hope for what is to come.

Some of us are too pragmatic for such a dream life. We plant our heels in the soil of reality and keep our hearts on a tight leash, careful, reasonable enough not to let them wander into such fanciful, unregulated territory. But this is no way for the hopeful people of God to live. With God, *all* things are possible (Matthew 19:26). Those who dream remember this, and so their hearts and minds can frolic in the hope of holy possibility. Their mouths can shout for joy and laughter can swell in their chests because the dreamers know that hope is what sustains us in the waiting.

> He who goes out weeping, bearing the seed for sowing, shall come home with shouts of joy, bringing his sheaves with him (Psalm 126:5-6).

Yes, we wait during Advent. We shift anxious with anticipation for the coming King. We prepare and plan and plot our next steps, diligently living each day as it comes, but sometimes, forgetting that though we wait, we are invited to dream. We are prodded towards hoping against all that our eyes see, for the heaven that is already here in our midst. Thy kingdom come. It has, it is, it will again. Might we celebrate the fervent faithfulness of God, the restoration already given through Jesus and the coming restoration of the earth like dreamers do, with shouts of joy, with visions of hope, with laughter on our lips?

Let Advent be not only a contemplative time, but a spirited celebration of the joy of the already-here Jesus.

A Question For Reflection In The Waiting

What are the things God is inviting me to dream about again?

Jesu, joy of man's desiring, you remind us that a joyful heart gives life to the bones. Your Word continually flashes the bright bold banner of hope, even when circumstances seem dark. Through slavery and defeat, through discipline and correction, through confession and redemption you continue to whisper hope in every story. Come, Lord Jesus, fill our hearts with the joy of this everlasting hope. Teach us to dream and laugh and celebrate in our anxious waiting for you.

12

DECEMBER 12: HE WILL SURELY DO IT

Today's Reading

Rejoice always, pray without ceasing, give thanks in all
circumstances; for this is the will of God in Christ Jesus
for you. Do not quench the Spirit. Do not despise
prophecies, but test everything; hold fast what is good.
Abstain from every form of evil.
Now may the God of peace himself sanctify you
completely, and may your whole spirit and soul and body
be kept blameless at the coming of our Lord Jesus Christ.
He who calls you is faithful; he will surely do it.

55

1 Thessalonians 5:16-24

He Will Surely Do It

With everything else this season requires of us, God instructs us to pray without ceasing. It's not only our continual prayer that He calls us to, but a continual position of gratitude. Give thanks in all circumstances, Paul reminds. *All* circumstances. This is surely easier said than practiced. A pray-without-ceasing-with-an-attitude-of-gratitude lifestyle takes intentional effort and cultivation. Most of us do not inhabit this space by default and without work.

To pray this way, we have to turn from our traditional view of prayer, where we sit still with folded hands and closed eyes for a time. To live out the prayer described here requires that our very lives essentially become a prayer. We have to become aware of our need, our complete and utter inability to create for ourselves the life God intends for us. Only in true humility can we learn what it looks like to pray without ceasing. This kind of prayer can only come from recognizing and confessing our insufficiency when it comes to living life on our own terms. We need God's help, every hour, so we may discover in this recognition of our tremendous need, what it means to pray without ceasing. This understanding of the depth of our lack creates in us the ability to offer gratitude in *all* circumstances. One thing leads to another, for this is the will of God in Christ Jesus for you (1 Thessalonians 5:18).

The holly-jolly anthems of the carols we hear as we wander through the shops and ride around in our cars providing a cheerful, idealistic backdrop to this season of perpetual hope. Advent seems like a season where it ought to be easy to hold onto good things, to "behave ourselves". How often have we heard a parent admonish an antsy, over-eager child in the checkout lines at the store to "be good", lest they lose out on gifts beneath the tree. Even if this isn't our own theology, it is none the less the theme of our culture's Christmas. Behave, Santa is watching. But Santa is not watching–God is. And God knows full-well that we struggle to "be good," so He invites us to pray without ceasing, to invite Him constantly into every moment of our lives that we might manage to learn a different obedience. The kind that says, Lord I cannot do it in my own strength, help me to do it in yours.

As we wait, as we struggle to prepare the way for Christ's coming, we are no more capable of willing ourselves into perfection or resolute faithfulness than we are any other season of the year. We *need* Jesus for this. Paul Miller wrote, "Prayer is a moment of incarnation – God with us. God involved in the details of my life."[7] Our inability, our forever-struggle is precisely why He came, and is coming again. And so we cry out on repeat, through a life of prayerfulness, every hour, come, Lord Jesus, hear our prayer!

Now may the God of peace himself sanctify you
completely, and may your whole spirit and soul and body
be kept blameless at the coming of our Lord Jesus
Christ. He who calls you is faithful; he will surely do it (1
Thessalonians 5:23).

How can we be kept blameless for the coming of Jesus? Through the continual sanctification that comes when one's life becomes a prayerful one. As we learn to pray without ceasing, when we give continual thanks, the Sprit of God rests fully within our hearts and through His filling we are sanctified—made holy and blameless. Not by our effort, but by the indwelling presence of God. This is how He prepares us for His coming. Transformation like this cannot be achieved in our own strength, by our own effort. He will surely do it.

A Question For reflection In The Waiting
In what ways do I find prayer challenging?

God you have called us into a continual conversation that began at the moment of our birth. You have generously invited us into your constant presence through prayer and your Holy Spirit. Help us to enter into this mindful prayerfulness, to learn what it is to experience your incarnation every hour of our lives. Thank you for this gift, for the love you have for us, that you would do this for us, again and again, every hour we call to you. Come, Lord Jesus, teach us what it is to live in this sacred conversation with you.

13

DECEMBER 13: BEAR WITNESS ABOUT THE LIGHT

Today's Reading

There was a man sent from God, whose name was John. He came as a witness, to bear witness about the light, that all might believe through him. He was not the light, but came to bear witness about the light.

And this is the testimony of John, when the Jews sent priests and Levites from Jerusalem to ask him, "Who are you?" He confessed, and did not deny, but confessed, "I am not the Christ."

And they asked him, "What then? Are you Elijah?"

He said, "I am not."

"Are you the Prophet?"

And he answered, "No."

So they said to him, "Who are you? We need to give an answer to those who sent us. What do you say about yourself?"

He said, "I am the voice of one crying out in the wilderness, 'Make straight the way of the Lord,' as the prophet Isaiah said."

(Now they had been sent from the Pharisees.) They asked him, "Then why are you baptizing, if you are neither the Christ, nor Elijah, nor the Prophet?"

John answered them, "I baptize with water, but among you stands one you do not know, even he who comes after me, the strap of whose sandal I am not worthy to untie."

These things took place in Bethany across the Jordan, where John was baptizing.

John1:6-8, 19-28

Bear Witness About The Light

God could have sent Jesus to earth without any warning. He could have simply appeared one day, wandered into town and begun His ministry without any preparation or announcement. And yet, God chose a different way to send us our Savior. Jesus' arrival was the fulfillment of a long-awaited prophesy.

John, Jesus' cousin, served in a long line of prophets

all tasked with a similar mission: prepare the way, bear witness about the Light–tell the people about Jesus' coming. John came to help people make room in their hearts for the salvation they had heard about and hoped for, for generations. By his preaching and baptizing in the wilderness, He bore witness about Jesus.

In Advent, as in Lent, we make room in our hearts for Jesus to fill us. We remember the story from the beginning, retracing the missteps of Adam and Eve in the Garden, the continual rebellion of God's chosen people in the wilderness, the wandering years, the generations of bad kings, the hunger for justice and the failed attempts by man to uphold it. We recount the chronic waywardness of the human heart, the tendency towards backsliding and the reality that all of life apart from God is an unbearable struggle.

Cleaning our homes and adorning them with decorations, we prepare for the season. But these are only exterior representations of the interior work of the Holy Spirit who works inside of each of us, cleaning out our hearts and making room for Jesus to dwell. The waiting during Advent reminds us of how desperately we need a Savior. Advent reminds us of how dark it is, without His Light.

Then why are you baptizing, if you are neither the Christ, nor Elijah, nor the Prophet?" (John 6:24).

John's baptism ministry served as a call to repentance. Through baptism by water, John washed the people of their sins in preparation for the washing we would receive through the blood of Christ. John knew who he was, what he had been called to do, and he offered his service out of obedience.

> He was not the light, but came to bear witness about the light (John 6:8).

Jesus came and announced to us, "I am the light of the world. Whoever follows me will not walk in darkness, but will have the light of life" (John 8:12). During His sermon on the mount, Jesus told the people, told us, that *we* are the light of the world (Matthew 5:14). How can this be, we wonder, how can Jesus and we both be "the light of the world"? This is made possible because our lives as believers are hidden in Christ. Our lives now grafted to His, allow us to be a light as He was. Christ's presence in us is reflected to the world through the living out of our active, sacrificial faith.

We too have been tasked with John's mission. We also bear witness about the light. By the indwelling of the Holy Spirit, received through baptism, we carry the message of hope within us–we carry His light in us. And "if we walk in the light, as he is in the light, we have fellowship with one another, and the blood of Jesus his Son cleanses us from all sin" (1 John 1:7).

A Question For Reflection In The Waiting
How can I bear the light of Christ today?

God, for generations whispers of your coming filtered throughout the earth. You sent your prophets to prepare the way, to help ready our hearts, to bear witness about the light, so that we would know that the darkness was not forever. Thank you for the opportunity for repentance, for the promise of restoration, for the brilliance of the Light of Christ, who shines in us and on us each day. Come, Lord Jesus. Help us to carry your truth, the Light of the world into the darkest corners, make us able to bear witness about your Light, that others might know the joy that we have been given in you.

14

DECEMBER 14: DWELLING PLACE

Today's Reading

Now when the king lived in his house and the Lord had given him rest from all his surrounding enemies, the king said to Nathan the prophet, "See now, I dwell in a house of cedar, but the ark of God dwells in a tent." And Nathan said to the king, "Go, do all that is in your heart, for the Lord is with you."

But that same night the word of the Lord came to Nathan, "Go and tell my servant David, 'Thus says the Lord: Would you build me a house to dwell in? I have not lived in a house since the day I brought up the people of Israel from Egypt to this day, but I have been moving about in a tent for my dwelling. In all places where I have moved with all the people of Israel, did I speak a word with any of the judges of Israel, whom I commanded to shepherd my people Israel, saying, "Why have you not built me a house of cedar?"' Now, therefore, thus you shall say to my servant David, 'Thus says the Lord of hosts, I took you from the pasture, from following the sheep, that you should be prince over my people Israel. And I have been with you wherever you went and have cut off all your enemies from before you. And I will make for you a great name, like the name of the great ones of the earth. And I will appoint a place for my people Israel and will plant them, so that they may dwell in their own place and be disturbed no more. And violent men shall afflict them no more, as formerly, from the time that I appointed judges over my people Israel. And I will give you rest from all your enemies. Moreover, the Lord declares to you that the Lord will make you a house. And your house and your kingdom shall be made sure forever before me. Your throne shall be established forever.'"

2 Samuel 7:1-11, 16

Dwelling Place

The arrhythmical thump of a hammer booms outside the walls of my new home, and with each thud, a new dwelling place takes its shape. Eventually, the current construction zone will become another home for someone, a spacious place for a couple or a family. Most of us want a permanent place to root, a place we can call home, where we settle into comfortable routines, where we find stability and sanctuary from the restless world beyond our front doors. We camp in tents for fun, not as a lifestyle. Most of us are not gypsies—even if we feel the occasional tug of wanderlust on our hearts.

Church seasons, like Advent, root us in a tradition ages older than ourselves, connecting us to a history of generational, celebratory worship in the church that has gone before us. Traditions like Advent give us a familiar place to dwell, a place that has long been settled before we wandered in and a place that will likely remain after we have wandered on to glory. The familiarity and routine of the practice comforts us, offering a stability when the rest of the world rocks and sways with discontent, terror, sickness, disease and chaos.

The Israelites knew what it was to wander, to lack a permanent home. Through repeated oppression, assault and upheaval, they lacked a territory to set down, to remain still, to dwell permanently. But not forever. God had promised them a dwelling place.

And I will appoint a place for my people Israel and will plant them, so that they may dwell in their own place and be disturbed no more (2 Samuel 7:10).

Indeed, God consecrated a Promise Land for His people, an actual plot of earth that could be walked and measured, a place where crops would grow, animals would graze, families would erect buildings and markets, where children would run and play. He set apart for them a land rich and fertile, abundant in goodness, not unlike the generosity of the first garden, *Eden*. But it would never be Eden. The path to perfection had been cut off, and so this new dwelling place would reflect both the fulfillment of God's promise and the shadow of the past. God never does the same thing twice. He is too big to work from a worn out playbook of repeats.

> Behold, I am doing a new thing; now it springs forth, do you not perceive it? I will make a way in the wilderness and rivers in the desert (Isaiah 43:19).

The new dwelling place God is calling His people to is not merely one of dust and grass, but a dwelling place called Christ. "Moreover, the Lord declares to you that the Lord will make you a house. And your house and your kingdom shall be made sure forever before me. Your throne shall be established forever" (2 Samuel 7:16). God selected David, a young boy from the fields to become part of the ancestral line of Jesus. God gave David the kingdom and home He promised and to the generations that followed from David. God established for us a way to dwell in Christ. Even before David, and before Jesus' birth, Moses said, Lord, you have been our dwelling place in all generations (Psalm 90:1).

In Advent, as we wait for our permanent dwelling place beside God, we can find our home in Jesus. He is the only sanctuary, the only home, the only place where we can find the stability and safety we hunger for. He is the place where our hearts find rest in all seasons–but most especially in the waiting.

A Question For Reflection In The Waiting
What does it mean to me to call Jesus my "dwelling place"?

Gracious God, how good you have been to your people from the beginning of time. Though we've wandered, you've never left us. You have always been the dwelling place for your people, even when home has seemed like an impossible dream. You sent your Son to make His home among us, and by His coming we have been invited to make our home in Him. Lord steady us as we wait for you. Help us over the threshold of our doubt and discouragement, of our not-enoughness, that keeps us standing on the outside of you. Come, Lord Jesus, help us to enter in and receive from you the rest our anxious souls crave.

15

DECEMBER 15: FAVOR

In the sixth month the angel Gabriel was sent from God to a city of Galilee named Nazareth, to a virgin betrothed to a man whose name was Joseph, of the house of David. And the virgin's name was Mary. And he came to her and said, "Greetings, O favored one, the Lord is with you!" But she was greatly troubled at the saying, and tried to discern what sort of greeting this might be. And the angel said to her, "Do not be afraid, Mary, for you have found favor with God. And behold, you will conceive in your womb and bear a son, and you shall call his name Jesus.

He will be great and will be called the Son of the Most High. And the Lord God will give to him the throne of his father David, and he will reign over the house of Jacob forever, and of his kingdom there will be no end."
And Mary said to the angel, "How will this be, since I am a virgin?"
And the angel answered her, "The Holy Spirit will come upon you, and the power of the Most High will overshadow you; therefore the child to be born will be called holy—the Son of God. And behold, your relative Elizabeth in her old age has also conceived a son, and this is the sixth month with her who was called barren. For nothing will be impossible with God." And Mary said, "Behold, I am the servant of the Lord; let it be to me according to your word." And the angel departed from her.
Luke 1:26-38

Favor

God's promise to give His people a permanent dwelling place includes the obedient participation of a young, unmarried woman. Chosen by God, the angel Gabriel calls Mary "favored"–chosen for this specific, monumental call, to be the mother of Jesus. This story is almost too fantastical to believe. But because of the prophesies of the Old Testament, because of the proven track record God has shown up to this moment, the selection of Mary, for this virgin birth, and spectacular calling somehow doesn't shock us all that much. After all, tracing Jesus' family tree reveals a genealogical litany of less than conventional choices to make up the lineage of the Holy King of heaven. God could have chosen anyone and repeatedly he chooses those whom we'd least expect. Mary responds obediently, "...let it be to me according to your word."

What kind of faith does it take to say "yes" to God's invitation to participate in His story? Aren't we a people who measure outcomes and statistics, who read reviews and ratings before we commit to anything, from buying a new refrigerator, to shelling out a few dollars to see the latest film? God's messenger called Mary "favored" and she responded with a willing "yes" to the shocking invitation presented to her. God forces us to reconcile the addition of yet another seemingly interesting addition to the Holy family tree. Mary, young, humble, and engaged to be married, willingly accepts God's plan, with no stipulations for the inevitable fall out this obedience will have on her own life. She surrenders fully, and the dwelling place of David begins to form in the secret place of her womb.

Saying yes to God will always mean more than we can possibly imagine.[8]

In Advent as we remember the wild obedience of young Mary, we hear the word, "favor" spoken over her, and are reminded that through God's choosing of her, by the inception of Jesus, the word, favor is spoken to us also. Through Jesus, God chooses us–He grafts us into the beautifully gnarled bark of His family tree. Through the flesh and blood of His Son He chooses us, His creation, for salvation. When we remember our own standing as one favored by God, aren't we that much more willing to say "yes" to what God has invited us into–even when it appears unconventional and dangerous? Knowing that we too bear the favor of God strengthens us to willingly embrace the unimaginable that He calls us to.

In Advent, as we wait, we need not wonder if He will pick us. He has already chosen us, through the blessing of Mary, and the blood of His Son. We don't know what this choosing will mean for our lives, where this honor will take us, but we can accept the title, *favored*, and live faithfully into all that it entails.

A Question For reflection In The Waiting
What does it mean to me to know that God chose me, that He chooses me still?

God you are generous without measure. How gracious you are to have chosen Mary, to choose us, to be your children. God help us to accept this grace, to embrace you as you embrace us. Teach us what it is to say "yes" again and again to the story you are writing with our lives. Come, Lord Jesus, help us to live faithfully in the calling as your favored children.

16

DECEMBER 16: STEADFAST LOVE

Today's Reading

I will sing of the steadfast love of the Lord, forever;
with my mouth I will make known your faithfulness to all
generations.
For I said, "Steadfast love will be built up forever;
in the heavens you will establish your faithfulness."
You have said, "I have made a covenant with my chosen
one;
I have sworn to David my servant:
'I will establish your offspring forever,

---

and build your throne for all generations.'"
Of old you spoke in a vision to your godly one, and said:
"I have granted help to one who is mighty;
I have exalted one chosen from the people.
I have found David, my servant;
with my holy oil I have anointed him,
so that my hand shall be established with him;
my arm also shall strengthen him.
The enemy shall not outwit him;
the wicked shall not humble him.
I will crush his foes before him
and strike down those who hate him.
My faithfulness and my steadfast love shall be with him,
and in my name shall his horn be exalted.
I will set his hand on the sea
and his right hand on the rivers.
He shall cry to me, 'You are my Father,
my God, and the Rock of my salvation.'
Psalm 89: 1-4, 19-26

Steadfast Love

Dietrich Bonhoeffer wrote, "Advent creates people. New people."[9] The newness we experience in Advent only comes because of the steadfast love of God. Because He loves us, God gives us this time, a season of waiting, which isn't passive at all. As we anticipate and prepare for Jesus' arrival, our hearts can't help but be transformed—we become new people, in the fullness of Jesus' presence. This is what God's steadfast love looks like in action. The generosity of the Advent season begs for us to notice the faithfulness of God. Seasonal hymns re-tell the story of our redemption, calling out the goodness of God for all people. Today's reading offers rich words of worship, proclaiming a small sampling of God's virtuous ways.Here, the psalmist reminds us that God has made a covenant, a promise of restoration. God has granted help, established a dwelling place, built a foundation and defeated the enemies of His people.

My faithfulness and my steadfast love shall be with him (Psalm 89:24).

Part of the promise Jesus embodies is the eternal presence of God's love for all time. We can't easily wrap our minds around God's immense love for us. How do we know He loves us? What proof do we have? Is His love defined by our blessings?– surely His love cannot rest solely on what we have, on what we can measure. How can we know anything about the love of God when the world sags with the weight of horrendous oppression and continual sin and despair? The answer of course, is Jesus. Jesus is how we know of God's steadfast love. Jesus, the God who became man, Jesus the King with the thorny crown pressed fitfully against His brow, Jesus, the living evidence of God's steadfast love, raised high on a cross for all to see, Jesus, raised from death that we might become new people–all because of a love that would not, and will not quit.

> "Only where God is can there be a new beginning. We cannot command God to grant it; we can only pray to God for it."[10]

Knowing the majesty of God–experiencing His glory during Advent implores our hearts to sing as the psalmist does here, of the continued faithfulness of God, who rather than rejecting us in our brokenness decides instead, to make us new. *New people*, all because of love. Renewed in spirit we can call out the goodness of God, we can re-tell the story of our salvation through worshipping God for His faithfulness.

A Question For Reflection In The Waiting
What does God's steadfast love look like in my life right now?

God, you love us with immeasurable generosity. There is nothing we have done, or can ever do that can earn us a share of the steadfast love that you pour out over your people generation to generation. Awash in your love, we are remade. Daily you shower us, and again and again we wake up to the newness of our redemption through Jesus. Come, Lord Jesus, help us to sing boldly in the showers of your love, telling everyone we meet about the spring of Living Water, who washes us clean.

17

DECEMBER 17: SING

"Sing, O barren one, who did not bear;
break forth into singing and cry aloud,
you who have not been in labor!
For the children of the desolate one will be more
than the children of her who is married," says the Lord.
"Enlarge the place of your tent,
and let the curtains of your habitations be stretched out;
do not hold back; lengthen your cords
and strengthen your stakes.
For you will spread abroad to the right and to the left,

---

and your offspring will possess the nations
and will people the desolate cities.
"Fear not, for you will not be ashamed;
be not confounded, for you will not be disgraced;
for you will forget the shame of your youth,
and the reproach of your widowhood you will remember
no more.
For your Maker is your husband,
the Lord of hosts is his name;
and the Holy One of Israel is your Redeemer,
the God of the whole earth he is called.
For the Lord has called you
like a wife deserted and grieved in spirit,
like a wife of youth when she is cast off,
says your God.
For a brief moment I deserted you,
but with great compassion I will gather you.
In overflowing anger for a moment
I hid my face from you,
but with everlasting love I will have compassion on you,"
says the Lord, your Redeemer.
"This is like the days of Noah to me:
as I swore that the waters of Noah
should no more go over the earth,
so I have sworn that I will not be angry with you,
and will not rebuke you.
For the mountains may depart
and the hills be removed,

---

but my steadfast love shall not depart from you,
and my covenant of peace shall not be removed,"
says the Lord, who has compassion on you.
Isaiah 54:1-10

Sing

The year we awoke to find our Christmas tree on its side, sappy water from the base soaking into the carpet and the floor littered with shards of broken glass, and a dusting of glitter, glistening in the dawn's early light, I had no song in my heart. What my eyes could perceive in those moments, was a monumental mess and the loss of some small treasures tenderly passed down through the years. All of it smashed and broken. Wet, disintegrating. Ruined. The room that had only days earlier been decorated and prepared, now resembling something akin to the aftermath or a small, indoor microburst. The only song I sang that morning bore the tune of lament, each verse sung in groans through lips pursed in frustration and twisted with disappointment.

The histories of God's people throughout the Old Testament include far worse devastation than a tipped tree, and broken glass. God's earliest people knew deep despair intimately. Circumstances had thoroughly searched them and found them repeatedly, to be both wayward *and* obedient,   resilient *and* corruptible. Faithful *and* faithless, often at the same time, or nearly so. But the beauty of these stories is that in them, we read our own history, we see our own struggle in a different time-frame, with different characters, but all of us still struggling towards God as He continues to call to us, through their stories, through our own.

> For the Lord has called you like a wife deserted and grieved in spirit, like a wife of youth when she is cast off (Isaiah 54:6).

Isaiah's words today begin with a joyful invitation–*Sing*, he encourages. He reminds us of where we have been, of the barrenness we have experienced for a season (for many seasons, perhaps) and then he recounts the good, faithfulness of God which is to be our anthem.

> This is like the days of Noah to me: as I swore that the waters of Noah should no more go over the earth, so I have sworn that I will not be angry with you, and will not rebuke you (Isiah 54:11).

Though our circumstances may appear difficult, though our trees and our lives fall down around us, our song must still rise. The steadfast love of God–the unending, unrelenting goodness of our Creator pours down over us, as it did in the manna from heaven. Our God moves with us still, as He did in the pillar and the smoke. Though struggle and strife occasionally pull the rug out from under us, and trials shatter our treasures, His steadfast love shall not depart from us (Isaiah 54:10), God reminds.

In all seasons, God implores us to sing *His* song, a song of mercy and redemption, of rescue and restoration. This is the covenant remembered in Advent, the long-suffering in the waiting for the once and final Hope to gather us to Himself. Sing! Sing! Do not hold back, (Isaiah 54:2) make room, Isaiah encourages. Go wherever God leads, without fear and hesitation for what may come.

Whatever our circumstances in the midst of the waiting, God invites us to keep singing. To keep going. To recall and treasure His proven faithfulness and to remember His deep, irrevocable compassion for us that came first in a manger, and then on a cross. Sing, for the Lord has called you.

A Question For Reflection In The Waiting
What song is my heart singing today?

God of all people, you generously gave us your Word on paper, in the flesh, that we would have a record of your love from the beginning. How quickly our circumstances and seasons of hard times tempt us to forget, to lose the words to our song. Remind us today, Lord, of the tune to which you have written our own story, put the words in our heart and help us to sing of your faithfulness, not only in Advent, but in all of the seasons that come after. Come, Lord Jesus let the waiting be a space for our growth, our healing, and our hope to prevail.

18

DECEMBER 18: A SIGN

Today's Reading

And the angel said to them, "Fear not, for behold, I bring you good news of great joy that will be for all the people. For unto you is born this day in the city of David a Savior, who is Christ the Lord. And this will be a sign for you: you will find a baby wrapped in swaddling cloths and lying in a manger." And suddenly there was with the angel a multitude of the heavenly host praising God and saying,
"Glory to God in the highest,

and on earth peace among those with whom he is
pleased!"
Luke 2:10-14

A Sign

Who among us isn't looking–even now–for a sign? How
many times have we lamented to a friend, if only we had
a "sign" to help us know what to do, or where to go?
Aren't our own prayers riddled with petitions to God for
a sign, some special signal that would help us? Signs from
God are biblical. Our request is not so ridiculous after
all. The fact is, we receive signs from God far more often
than we likely realize, but we miss them. Or we don't trust
them. In Gideon-like fashion, we flip our fleece repeatedly,
asking God for *one more* sign, just so we can be sure.

> And he said to him, "If now I have found favor in your
> eyes, then show me a sign that it is you who speak with me"
> (Judges 6:17).

In our waiting, we doubt. We forget God's recorded
faithfulness and distrust settles over our hearts. It's proof
that we're always wanting a sign that God is *for* us, that He
is present, moving, and not as silent as He seems to be.

When the angel appeared to the shepherds in the field,
he told them outright that "this would be a sign" for them.
What's the sign? The sudden appearance of an angel
would be a sufficient sign for any of us that something

important was happening. But the angel isn't the sign, the angel is only the messenger bringing news of the sign.

> And this will be a sign for you: you will find a baby wrapped in swaddling clothes and lying in a manger (vs. 12).

This is the good news the whole world has been waiting for. Since the 400 years of God's seeming silence at the close of the Old Testament, people everywhere have been waiting for a sign. Some bold, unmistakable clue that God has not completely abandoned and rejected them in finality. Of all the signs God could have sent, He selects His very own Son to be the sign of great joy, for all people. The sign and proof of His relentless love.

While Advent glitters and glows with the usual, seasonal trimmings, our hearts wrestle in the shadow of the long-awaited coming of Jesus. It is not unusual for us to feel a great distance between ourselves and the promise of salvation. After all, we live here, in the concrete fields of our time, shepherding our families and our own lives, feeling the nearness of danger always potentially around the next block or bend in the road. We look up, but cannot see the stars. We stand still, but the world spins and spins. Culture throws every possibly opportunity our direction, confusing our priorities and tempting us to distraction. We need a sign, a glaring reminder of who we are and where we are going. We want to know how we will get there–who will lead us?

Knowing what we needed, God sent the baby in the manger, Christ on the cross, Christ walking around in the days after death. Jesus, the eternal, living sign of God's immaculate love for us. Jesus, good news of great joy for all people. At the announcement of the birth of Jesus, all of heaven unleashes its praise.

Let our voices join the angels in singing, "glory to God in the highest," for our God has sent a sign for all people, a living hope for our once and for all salvation. He has sent us His very own Son.

A Question For Reflection In The Waiting
What signs am I seeking and waiting for this season?

Great God almighty, how mercifully you love us. You know our doubting ways and our constant need for the reminder of your everlasting love. You selected for us, the greatest sign of your promised mercy in Jesus, and offered Him to all people, to us, even though you knew we would reject Him. Help us to see the signs of your unending grace, Help us to trust you even when the sky looks empty, and we cannot see your face shining in the stars. Lord, God, eternal Light of heaven, turn our hearts to you this season, draw us to yourself, that we might savor the good news and taste the sweet joy of salvation. Come, Lord Jesus. Glory to you, God, in the highest.

19

DECEMBER 19: A BLESSING, A WARNING

Today's Reading

Behold, I send my messenger, and he will prepare the way before me. And the Lord whom you seek will suddenly come to his temple; and the messenger of the covenant in whom you delight, behold, he is coming, says the Lord of hosts. But who can endure the day of his coming, and who can stand when he appears? For he is like a refiner's fire and like fullers' soap. He will sit as a refiner and purifier of silver, and he will purify the sons of Levi and refine them like gold and silver, and they will bring offerings in

---

righteousness to the Lord. Then the offering of Judah and Jerusalem will be pleasing to the Lord as in the days of old and as in former years. Behold, I will send you Elijah the prophet before the great and awesome day of theLord comes. And he will turn the hearts of fathers to their children and the hearts of children to their fathers, lest I come and strike the land with a decree of utter destruction.

Malachi 3:1-4, 4:5-6

A Blessing, A Warning

Malachi, "God's Messenger," offers to us this day a good and difficult word, a blessing and a warning. The very Lord we seek and wait for will come–suddenly, just as we hope. But His coming will not be an easy one. We wait anxiously for Jesus but with the joy of His return, there will also be judgment. Jesus came and comes again, to seek and to save the lost, to judge the living and the dead.

> I charge you in the presence of God and of Christ Jesus, who is to judge the living and the dead, and by his appearing and his kingdom: preach the word; be ready in season and out of season (2 Timothy 4:2a).

Malachi's message to the Israelites was to ready themselves through repentance and worship for the coming of the Christ, and so it is our message as well. The Advent season, much like Lent, invites us to recall the blessings and warnings extended to our ancestors in the wilderness and ponder those truths, as Mary did, deep in our hearts. Not only to ponder, but to act. To believe that the blessings and warnings are for us too in this beginning season. The refining by way of the fuller's soap is a hard and "bruitiful" image of how God presses us clean.

In Malachi's day, in order to prepare and whiten woolen fabric, a fuller stretched the wool across a rock, and using a combination of plant ash, and clay and water, (the fuller's soap). Using a rock or piece of pottery, he would then scrape, mash and rub this "soap" into the fibers in order to clean the wool and fill out the fibers. If God refines us "like the fuller's soap"(Malachi 3:2), then we are the wool, stretched across the rock, doused with water and rubbed hard until we are full with a new and desirable purpose. Thoroughly cleansed of our impurities, by His refining, God makes us useful for the work of His kingdom.

This is not the Advent image that warms our hearts. The most recognizable image of Advent is the manger scene, the creche. Perhaps we envision a small glowing cave with Mary, Joseph and the shepherds bowed reverently, gazing serenely upon the freshly born baby King. But how many of us want to see the image that Malachi presents to us here–images of the Refiner's fire and the fuller's soap. Neither of these produces the warm, calm feeling that settles over us as we set out our nativity scenes across our mantles. In Advent, we don't often meditate on the fact that the mantle that Christ carried was a cross.

The purification of God is a blessing we can receive in any season, when we are willing. Our waiting hearts during Advent become a soft terrain in which God can set up camp and begin (or continue) the heart work of both the blessing and warning He extends to us. "I'm coming," He says, and "my coming will be difficult for you." When He comes, He will turn our hearts back towards each other, righting what sin has made crooked, restoring His creation and establishing His kingdom here–The promise of *Immanuel, God with us.* Let us not hide from His refining, or shrink back from the cross to the serenity of the manger. In Him we have both, the beautiful blessing of salvation, and the trial of redemption.

A Question For reflection In the Waiting
Where do I see the refining work of God in my life as I wait?

Generous God, how great thou art, that you would send your perfect, precious son to carry the cross, suffer and surrender to your will, for our sake. Help us to model this surrender and sacrifice in our own lives. Make us ready recipients and participants in your refining, that we would keep ever in our minds the purpose of the pain, the promise of resurrection with you, one day. No matter the difficulty, you are worthy. Come, Lord Jesus, it is only by your strength that we can surrender, all for your glory.

20

DECEMBER 20: MADE READY

Today's Reading

In the days of Herod, king of Judea, there was a priest
named Zechariah, of the division of Abijah. And he had a
wife from the daughters of Aaron, and her name was
Elizabeth. And they were both righteous before God,
walking blamelessly in all the commandments and
statutes of the Lord. But they had no child, because
Elizabeth was barren, and both were advanced in years.
Now while he was serving as priest before God when his
division was on duty, according to the custom of the
priesthood, he was chosen by lot to enter the temple of

---

the Lord and burn incense. And the whole multitude of
the people were praying outside at the hour of incense.
And there appeared to him an angel of the Lord standing
on the right side of the altar of incense. And Zechariah
was troubled when he saw him, and fear fell upon him.
But the angel said to him, "Do not be afraid, Zechariah,
for your prayer has been heard, and your wife Elizabeth
will bear you a son, and you shall call his name John. And
you will have joy and gladness, and many will rejoice at
his birth, for he will be great before the Lord. And he
must not drink wine or strong drink, and he will be filled
with the Holy Spirit, even from his mother's womb. And
he will turn many of the children of Israel to the Lord
their God, and he will go before him in the spirit and
power of Elijah, to turn the hearts of the fathers to the
children, and the disobedient to the wisdom of the just,
to make ready for the Lord a people prepared."
Luke 1:5-17

Made Ready

Sometimes our barrenness has nothing to do with our
physical circumstance and everything to do with our
paper-thin heart. The thing that stops us from believing
the miracle isn't only our advanced maturity, but also our
inability to imagine the impossible. We're too old for the
foolish imaginations run-rampant that we see in children.
Too wise in our own right, to dream fanciful dreams of the
impossible-made-possible. We know better–we've lived

hard times, our experiences fill us with doubt or, what we deem to be, a healthy measure of realism. We plant our feet in the solid earth and declare the miracle to be impossible. Absurd at best. We pray in our disbelief and sometimes, God hushes us with His holiness, in order to restore us.

Zechariah and his wife had prayed for years for a child. But after the long silence of God, they no longer believed the miracle was possible. Who among us hasn't lost hope when we've prayed long but heard only the hollows of our own voice? In the presence of God's angel, Zechariah became troubled, overcome with fear. The news that a son was to be nestled in the barren place within Elizabeth, seemed too ridiculous to be believed. He has real life to rely on, long hard evidence of experience that seemed more honest than the prophetic blessing extended by God's messenger. With his feet planted in the dry soil of reality, Zechariah found this message was too beautiful to be real.

> Embracing mystery demands that we refuse to stand over our history, examining it and judging it with aloof, sterile detachment.[11]

It's precisely in the hardened soil of our disbelief that God plants and waters the seeds of the miraculous. The mystery of His majesty unfurls lush and evergreen in the white-hot blaze of our doubt and disbelief. We can't make sense of it, and yet the miracle blooms in spite of all that seems opposed to its reality. In spite of even ourselves, who fight to believe in the goodness of God who allows suffering for years only to demand our faith in a moment. Zechariah had prayed, and doubted, and all but given up believing in the possibility of the impossible, and in a moment, God silences him for months because his doubt was bigger than his faith. *What kind of God is this?* We wonder.

Wonder. That's what we lose in our doubt. The wonder of God is the holy imagination that believes in the miraculous. The faith that embraces mystery without evidence or proof, but purely relies on the promises of God that have been spoken into our hearts for generations. In our prayers, we wander more than we wonder. And yet God continually invites us back to Himself. His truth calls us to forget the history that we have lived, and face forward, expectant, hopeful (Philippians 3:13), believing that God can and does transform barren places of hopelessness into fertile fields of salvation.

Zechariah's prayers were answered. God was sending someone to make ready the people for the coming Christ. Zechariah needed to do nothing but believe. God invited him to hope, to witness the miracle of God's mission from the very first row—as the father of the great messenger, John. All of Advent reminds us that God is making us ready. The waiting, the hoping—it all points us to the miracle unfolding, the grace of God that comes into our barrenness and fills the space with Himself. The mercy of the Savior who comes to raise us up with Him, in life and in death.

He will go before him in the spirit and power of Elijah, to turn the hearts of the fathers to the children, and the disobedient to the wisdom of the just, to make ready for the Lord a people prepared (Luke 1:17).

A Question For Reflection In The Waiting
What hope have I given up on?

Gracious God, how good you are to us. How patient and loving you are, though we doubt and dismiss the miracle of mercy in our lives again and again. You have given us all that we need, you prepare our hearts daily, renewing our faith and restoring our hope. Help us acknowledge your faithful presence in all of our moments. Help us to receive your message, though we are tempted to laugh in disbelief. Come, Lord Jesus, make us ready for you. Prepare our restless hearts, we pray.

21

DECEMBER 21: NO END OF PEACE

———

Todays's Reading

But there will be no gloom for her who was in anguish. In
the former time he brought into contempt the land of
Zebulun and the land of Naphtali, but in the latter time
he has made glorious the way of the sea, the land beyond
the Jordan, Galilee of the nations.
The people who walked in darkness
have seen a great light;
those who dwelt in a land of deep darkness,
on them has light shone.

———

COME LORD JESUS

You have multiplied the nation;
you have increased its joy;
they rejoice before you
as with joy at the harvest,
as they are glad when they divide the spoil.
For the yoke of his burden,
and the staff for his shoulder,
the rod of his oppressor,
you have broken as on the day of Midian.
For every boot of the tramping warrior in battle tumult
and every garment rolled in blood
will be burned as fuel for the fire.
For to us a child is born,
to us a son is given;
and the government shall be upon his shoulder,
and his name shall be called
Wonderful Counselor, Mighty God,
Everlasting Father, Prince of Peace.
Of the increase of his government and of peace
there will be no end,
on the throne of David and over his kingdom,
to establish it and to uphold it
with justice and with righteousness
from this time forth and forevermore.
The zeal of the Lord of hosts will do this.
Isaiah 9:1-7

No End Of Peace

Waiting sometimes feels like sitting alone in the dark. When will the light finally come, we wonder? The dawn of a new day comes slowly, with a gradual lightening of the sky. With every blink the sky seems to brighten, but it does not happen in an instant. We perceive the sunrise in incremental stanzas until the fullness of light overwhelms the last ribbons of darkness, and we realize we are now standing in the full brightness of a new day.

> The people who walked in darkness have seen a great light; those who dwelt in a land of deep darkness, on them has light shone (Isiah 9:2).

Though the Light of the World, (Christ), appears to be slow in His coming, His light does not meander into the world like the slow rising dawn. His coming, long foretold, is quickly realized as He slips out into a dim cave, in the night of a waiting world so long blanketed in shadow and darkness. He comes to us in that long-awaited moment awakening our hearts to Himself, as if someone has suddenly raised the shades. Our Light has come. And with His coming, all of the happenings of the dark shall cease.

Fallen governments, the oppressors, the booted warriors who trample the lives of the innocent and the widow, the crooked justice of man, the people who have made their home and their dealings tucked within the folds of great darkness, the restlessness of those who lack joy, those in anguish and despair –He will transform it all.

His perfect Light breaks and in the fullness of it, no evil thing can stand. Wickedness will not prevail, the darkness will not have the final say.

Wonderful Counselor, Mighty God, Everlasting Father, Prince of Peace (vs. 6).

His names implore us to rejoice for what He has accomplished, for what we have yet to see Him accomplish in our lifetimes. Wonderful, Mighty, Everlasting — hope-filled names for the Savior whose light overcomes the pitch black of the waiting world. How hungry we have been for this permanent Dawn. How expectantly we wait. With Jesus there will be no end of peace. This is our hope in the waiting of Advent, this promise of permanent peace in the person of Jesus.

A Question For Reflection In The Waiting
Where do I need God's peace in my life right now?

Mighty God, Everlasting Father, thank you for the light you shine in the dark, for the justice you execute according to your good and right nature, according to your love. You are faithful to come, not slow like the dawn, but with the urgency of a Father set on the merciful rescue of His children. Come, Lord Jesus, help us to wait for you with hope, to look forward to the peace that will not end, to trust in your righteousness, when our eyes still see only darkness.

22

DECEMBER 22: AGAIN I WILL SAY, REJOICE

Today's Reading

Rejoice in the Lord always; again I will say, rejoice. Let your reasonableness be known to everyone. The Lord is at hand; do not be anxious about anything, but in everything by prayer and supplication with thanksgiving let your requests be made known to God. And the peace of God, which surpasses all understanding, will guard your hearts and your minds in Christ Jesus.

Philippians 4:4-7

Again I Will Say, Rejoice

Several years ago, the results of a survey reported that 45% of people who responded actually dread the Christmas season. During the holidays, reports of depression or increased anxiety are up during the month of December. A quick Google search for "anxiety at Christmas time" returned over 18 million results. It seems the festive season of Advent, for many, is not an easy season for rejoicing. But Paul's word to the people at Philippi (and to us) here is "rejoice...do not be anxious about anything." Worship to combat worry. It's effective, but it isn't easy. When our anxiety levels are high, our first response is rarely to worship. Rising anxiety levels set off a whole chain of events in our hearts and minds and typically, worship isn't the first, second or third response. To worship during seasons of worry takes more effort than most of us can muster. It takes holy intervention to turn our hearts towards praise rather than our problems. But God is always willing to woo us. He is always wanting our heart's full attention.

Rather than wring our hands with worry, Paul encourages us to bring it all before God in prayer, humbly and "with thanksgiving (Philippians 4:6)." God's response to our prayers? Peace. When we surrender our fear and worry, God's inexplicable peace becomes the guard of our hearts and minds.

Rejoice in the Lord always; again I say rejoice (Philippians 4:4).

Paul offers what looks like a prescriptive solution to relieve our anxiety: rejoice, pray with gratitude, receive God's peace. And yet, our Advent season of waiting remains tinted with the gray of worry. So many of us struggle to come out from beneath the blues. Peace is what we want, hope is what we need to cling to, but finding peace can seem like a treacherous crossing of an icy sidewalk in winter. We tread cautiously, tense, waiting — expecting even, to fall.

Bring it *all* to God, Paul tells us–prayerfully, humbly, and with thanksgiving. Rejoice–celebrate in the waiting. Let God fill you with His joy and His inexplicable peace. The peace of God is a shield for our hearts protecting us from the enemy's efforts to discourage and dissuade us, keeping us from the depths of despair and driving us back from the edge of distraction. The act of rejoicing, even in our discomfort, guards not only our hearts from anxiety and fear, but our minds as well, keeping doubt and fear in check and not giving them the run of the place.

Come on your knees. Come humble, low, thanking God for His goodness in the waiting. Bless His name in the dark remembering that He is your Light, the hope of your salvation, the peace of your heart and the protector of your mind and your soul.

For our heart is glad in him, because we trust in his holy name (Psalm 33:21).

As we make our way to the manger, with each remaining step through the season of Advent, we can practice rejoicing. We can "tune our hearts to sing His praise"[12].

"As we wait and pray, God weaves his story and creates a wonder. Instead of drifting between comedy (denial) and tragedy (reality), we have a relationship with the living God, who is intimately involved with the details of our worlds. We are learning to watch for the story to unfold, to wait for the wonder.[13]"

A Question For Reflection In The Waiting
What worries and anxieties are currently robbing me of wonder?

Most magnificent God, you are so much bigger than our worries and anxiety. You are capable of managing all that distresses us, and in fact are steadily at work in our worry, even when our eyes cannot detect your presence. Teach us "some melodious sonnet," some tune of heaven that we can sing in this season, to bless your name, to rejoice in the mercy and grace of the manger, the hope of our Savior born unto us. Come, Lord Jesus, teach us to rejoice!

23

DECEMBER 23: GOD IS IN YOUR MIDST

Today's Reading

Sing aloud, O daughter of Zion;
shout, O Israel!
Rejoice and exult with all your heart,
O daughter of Jerusalem!
The Lord has taken away the judgments against you;
he has cleared away your enemies.
The King of Israel, the Lord, is in your midst;
you shall never again fear evil.
On that day it shall be said to Jerusalem:

"Fear not, O Zion;
let not your hands grow weak.
The Lord your God is in your midst,
a mighty one who will save;
he will rejoice over you with gladness;
he will quiet you by his love;
he will exult over you with loud singing.
Zephaniah 3:14-17

God Is In Your Midst

It's a strange thing to live in a story that already has a known ending. Though our lives unfold fresh and new to us each day, God has already seen the breadth of our days and knows how each moment will unfold. Tragedy and triumph alike. Every page of our life has already been accounted for and yet for us here on the ground level, every moment is new and unknown. That which is, already has been; that which is to be, already has been; and God seeks what has been driven away (Ecclesiastes 3:15). We know very little about our own lives–how long we have here, what will happen along the way. But God is seeking us. Actively. Passionately. Intentionally.

We wait for Jesus, and yet He has already come. His presence through the gift of the Holy Spirit, our invisible helper, remains with us, not only with but *within* those who believe. Jesus told His disciples, "and I will ask the Father, and he will give you another Helper, to be with you forever, even the Spirit of truth, whom the world cannot receive, because it neither sees him nor knows him. You know him, for he dwells with you and will be in you (John 14:16-17)."

He dwells with us *and* within us, but still, we wait for His coming. This is not an easy idea to understand, and this is what we mean when Christians describe living in the "already and not yet." We are encouraged here not to grow weary, not to let our hands go limp and weak in the work that God has given us to do in the meantime. He has tasked us with a purpose; go therefore and make disciples–go, tell people about Jesus. Invite others to open their eyes to the story they too are living in, whether they acknowledge it or not. Our King, whom we wait for, is already in our midst. He is currently at work writing the story that's already been written. Our prayers, our worship, and our outreach are one of the ways we get to participate in this fantastic epic unfolding. The Lord is in your midst (Zephaniah 3:15)–Heaven touching earth.

Not only is God among us, but He is singing over us. Loudly. Can you hear Him? Can you hear the sweet song of heaven crescendo over your life? His love quiets us, as He sings His love song over His creation. He has made everything beautiful, and He loves what he has made.

He has made everything beautiful in its time. Also, he has put eternity into man's heart, yet so that he cannot find out what God has done from the beginning to the end. I perceived that there is nothing better for them than to be joyful and to do good as long as they live (Ecclesiastes 3:11).

There is nothing better for us than to be joyful; rejoice and exult with all your heart, Zephaniah tells us. Advent, our waiting season is to be a season of celebration. This is a season for us to listen for His song over us. For us to offer our own song back to Him. A time to let the love of God, which flows down from heaven, which is embodied by Jesus and in us, through the Holy Spirit, to fill our hearts with His praise.

God is in our midst! He is among us now, serenading us with the song of heaven; a song for which we do not know the words, but the Holy Spirit within us, tunes our hearts to sing along. *Alleluia*, He is here.

A Question For Reflection In The Waiting
What song do I hear God singing over me today?

Lover of our souls, great God Almighty, your song is too sweet for us to bear. Your merciful tune, your lyrics of love fall all around us as we live in this tension of the already and not yet. Tune our ears to the melody of your great redemption, teach our hearts the chords to the hymn of heaven, and open us up to receive your tremendous love.

Quiet us, God, that we can hear you, steady us in the work of the not yet. Come, Lord Jesus, we want to hear the song of our Savior's birth, teach us the great ballad of His life, offered for us.

24

DECEMBER 24: IMMANUEL, GOD WITH US

Today's Reading

The book of the genealogy of Jesus Christ, the son of
David, the son of Abraham.

Abraham was the father of Isaac, and Isaac the father of
Jacob, and Jacob the father of Judah and his brothers, and
Judah the father of Perez and Zerah by Tamar, and Perez
the father of Hezron, and Hezron the father of Ram, and
Ram the father of Amminadab, and Amminadab the
father of Nahshon, and Nahshon the father of Salmon,
and Salmon the father of Boaz by Rahab, and Boaz the

---

father of Obed by Ruth, and Obed the father of Jesse, and Jesse the father of David the king.

And David was the father of Solomon by the wife of Uriah, and Solomon the father of Rehoboam, and Rehoboam the father of Abijah, and Abijah the father of Asaph, 8and Asaph the father of Jehoshaphat, and Jehoshaphat the father of Joram, and Joram the father of Uzziah, and Uzziah the father of Jotham, and Jotham the father of Ahaz, and Ahaz the father of Hezekiah, and Hezekiah the father of Manasseh, and Manasseh the father of Amos, and Amos the father of Josiah, and Josiah the father of Jechoniah and his brothers, at the time of the deportation to Babylon.

And after the deportation to Babylon: Jechoniah was the father of Shealtiel, and Shealtiel the father of Zerubbabel, and Zerubbabel the father of Abiud, and Abiud the father of Eliakim, and Eliakim the father of Azor, and Azor the father of Zadok, and Zadok the father of Achim, and Achim the father of Eliud, 15and Eliud the father of Eleazar, and Eleazar the father of Matthan, and Matthan the father of Jacob, and Jacob the father of Joseph the husband of Mary, of whom Jesus was born, who is called Christ.

So all the generations from Abraham to David were fourteen generations, and from David to the deportation to Babylon fourteen generations, and from the deportation to Babylon to the Christ fourteen generations. Now the birth of Jesus Christ took place in this way. When his mother Mary had been betrothed to Joseph, before they came together she was found to be with child from the Holy Spirit. And her husband Joseph, being a just man and unwilling to put her to shame, resolved to divorce her quietly. But as he considered these things, behold, an angel of the Lord appeared to him in a dream, saying, "Joseph, son of David, do not fear to take Mary as your wife, for that which is conceived in her is from the Holy Spirit. She will bear a son, and you shall call his name Jesus, for he will save his people from their sins." All this took place to fulfill what the Lord had spoken by the prophet:

"Behold, the virgin shall conceive and bear a son,
and they shall call his name Immanuel" (which means,
God with us). When Joseph woke from sleep, he did as
the angel of the Lord commanded him: he took his wife,
but knew her not until she had given birth to a son. And
he called his name Jesus.

Matthew 1: 1-25

Immanuel, God With Us

Jesus' family tree looks a lot like most of our own genealogical histories. We have the imperfect humanity of his ancestry recorded for all of time. We know their stories. We recognize their strengths and their sins. We see their triumphs and stumbling in our own histories, in ourselves. And yet this is the tree from which God specifically chose to send forth the Savior of the World. A perfect white Lamb descendant from a flock deckled with black sheep. We scratch our heads in wonder. God never does anything the way we expect. He always chooses the unlikely path, the path which so often looks like the one of *most* resistance.

And so it was with Jesus' own birth as well. The beauty of the unconventional incarnation of Christ is that it gives us a glimpse of the lengths God is always willing to go for His wandering children. God knows intimately the shape of our own family tree, the crooked bends in our very own branches, and so He sends us a rescuer from a gnarled and mighty tree of His own design. God's inclusion of common people who struggled with the same things we would inevitably struggle with, reveals a measure of His compassion for those of us who repeatedly struggle to get it right. God shows us here that He sees us, in all of our brokenness and he understands — He loves us still. And so He sent us Jesus, whose history looks comfortably like our own. God's divine intention is not thwarted by our frailty. It is precisely within these constraints that God shows up perfectly and rescues us from ourselves.

We want something glossier than a young woman, carrying the incarnate baby not of her husband, something less messy than the King of creation born into the manure of a sin-sick world, yet this is precisely the story we have. God with us, right here in the awkward, wayward world.

Immanuel, who didn't wait for us to clean ourselves up for His coming, but rather came to us, through the very womb of humanity, wearing the slick vernix of creation, tethered by the umbilical cord that extended all the way to heaven. Here, into the dry straw of the dusty earth He descended, uncurling His holy hands to grasp the imperfect, sin-stained fingers of humanity. This is the good news of Christmas–the gift we receive again and again in all of life's advent seasons. God with us. Right here. Right now.

Let's not hurry through this night. Let us sit awhile beside the manger in the muck of the stable, in the mess of our actual lives and soak in the glory of this truth. Immanuel. He is here. Even as we wait for His final coming, He is present. Sit still for a few minutes where you are. Can you feel Him beside you? Can you sense His mercy for you; can you hear the love He sings down over you? Listen — His life is in you. Let the rhythm of your heart fall in sync with the pulse of heaven.

A Question For Reflection In The Waiting
In what ways do I allow preoccupation with my imperfections to keep me from experiencing God's love for me, just as I am?

Good and glorious Jesus, you are here. You came willingly into our stinking mess and made your home here. You, the very Word made flesh, dwelling right here among us, not to condemn but to save, to rescue, to restore. Immanuel, here and now, in our lives, just as they are. Though we reject you, you remain. Though our family tree, our very own branch curls and bends with the weight of our sin, you descend, you lift the weight of waiting and carry the whole of creation on your shoulders. Come, Lord Jesus, make your residence in us today. You are our forever and always living Hope.

25

DECEMBER 25: YOUR GOD REIGNS

———

Today's Reading

How beautiful upon the mountains
are the feet of him who brings good news,
who publishes peace, who brings good news of happiness,
who publishes salvation,
who says to Zion, "Your God reigns."
The voice of your watchmen—they lift up their voice;
together they sing for joy;
for eye to eye they see
the return of the Lord to Zion.

———

Break forth together into singing,
you waste places of Jerusalem,
for the Lord has comforted his people;
he has redeemed Jerusalem.
The Lord has bared his holy arm
before the eyes of all the nations,
and all the ends of the earth shall see
the salvation of our God.
Isaiah 52:7-10

Your God Reigns

At last, this day is here. We've waited anxiously, expectantly, fighting for hope and joy all along the way but now the news spreads like wildfire. Today we celebrate our Savior.

Today, we remember His promise fulfilled. *And I will lead the blind in a way that they do not know, in paths that they have not known I will guide them. I will turn the darkness before them into light, the rough places into level ground. These are the things I do, and I do not forsake them* (Isaiah 42:16).

Neither our blindness, nor our wrestle with doubt, nor our penchant for forgetting our God can keep us from His love. Through Jesus, God has given us new eyes to see, a new heart to receive His love, to love Him in return, to love others, as He has loved us all. We were blind but now? *Now* we see. The blazing Light of the World shines and the darkness has not, cannot and will *not ever* overcome it. This is the good news we were promised–our hope fulfilled.

In the garden we turned our backs, we filled our stomachs and our hearts with the fruit of our own evil desires and live daily with the aching hole that our sin has eaten away in us, our God-shaped cavern, leaving us longing to be filled forever, for good. Now, the watchmen, and all the hosts of heaven proclaim for us the fulfillment of the greatest promise ever made:

I will never leave you nor forsake you (Joshua 1:5).

We are redeemed by the birth of God, in Jesus, here among us. Right here in our midst. Right here in the corrupted garden of His creation, he descends, offering us fresh hope, restored vision, making us new–filling our terrible heart-hole. Today, in celebration of this beautiful gift, we raise our voices in praise for what God has done. He has come for the whole earth, for all of creation. The trees of the field clap their hands, the angels of heaven sing praises to His name and we here, His beloved people, with our feet in the muck of the earth, leap like calves from our stalls at the unfailing goodness of God, who saw us before we were formed, who set in motion a plan to reunite us with Himself, as we were always intended to be.

It's Christmas day, Jesus has come to us, now and for all time. All of the ends of the earth shall see the salvation of

God (vs. 10). Your God reigns today, from this day forward, into eternity, He is enthroned in His Kingdom, the Kingdom of God, right here in our midst.

The celebration of this day will wane at sunset, the last candle on the advent wreath will puff out and its light turn to gray smoke, wafting towards heaven, disappearing right before your eyes. But the Light of Christ will not go out. The Light of this day will burn without a flicker, steady into the coming days and years according to the kairos of God. As you lay down in your bed tonight, you can recall the faithfulness of God that extends beyond a small boxed day on the calendar into the hearts of His people for all time. Our King has come. We will sleep in peace this day, remembering the mercy of the manger.

A Question For Reflection In The Waiting
How does the promise of Christmas, of Immanuel, *God with us,* help me to live hopefully with the weight of waiting?

Good and gracious God, through the gift of Jesus, you have set eternity in our hearts. You came down to us, lowering yourself here, calling us friend, and making a way for us to be with you again. You love us with an everlasting love that we neither deserve nor can comprehend, but can only accept, by your good grace. Our hearts can scarcely contain the goodness of your love. You overwhelm us with your Holy affinity for the people you have made. Turn our hearts ever towards you today and in the coming days, when the decorations are gone, and life slips into the familiar rhythms of our routines. Come, Lord Jesus. Make your home in us. Teach us to wait for you alone, to trust patiently, and with unfailing hope in your promise of eternal resurrection with you.

Acknowledgements

My name may be on the bottom of the front cover, and listed on the sales page, but the reality is, there's a whole host of saints who have held my hand and held me up during the writing, editing and release of this book. Without their prayers, encouragement, pep-talks, keen eye for type-o's and general moral support, I'd have probably filed this project away for another time.

To my friends Sarah and Susan, your sharp editor-eyes have saved me from numerous misplaced commas and a whole host of other grammatical catastrophes. This book is better for having passed through your hands.

To my beautiful GraceTable writing team, thank you for baring with me while I dropped numerous balls during the writing of this book. Your grace and support is a testimony of Jesus in you. I say it because I mean it, you are the best people on the internet.

To my dear "bosom friend" Christine (to borrow a phrase from L.M. Montgomery), thank you. Your friendship blesses me more than I could ever begin to express here. That is a book of its own. Your cover art for this book is tremendous and the spirit in which you continually give inspires me.

To my writing mentors and dear friends, Jennifer Lee, Christin Ditchfield, Michelle DeRusha, and Shelly Miller, you've each been a source of tremendous wisdom, encouragement and prayer support when I have needed you. Your generosity is unmatched. I can't believe how good God is, that He has placed you in my life, *for such a time as this.*

To my indie publishing gurus, Shawn Smucker, Andi Cumbo-Floyd and Ed Cyzewski, I say a hearty thanks. You three are a gift to writers and readers everywhere. I am forever grateful for the way you mentor and invite. You set the bar very high, my friends.

To my street team, I wasn't kidding when I told you that I couldn't do this without you. Thank you for stepping up, offering your feedback, help encouragement and prayers, and for helping spread the word about this book. You made something difficult feel like a gift.

To my children, thank you. You endured many late breakfasts on account of me being lost in this work. You guys are my most favorites. I pray this book helps you to keep Jesus in your heart not only in Advent, but always.

To my husband, you listen patiently every time I come to you and tell you that "I feel God saying..." and then you move heaven and earth to afford me the time and space I need to walk through whatever wild vision God has hatched in me, in that season. I could not do this without you.

Finally, I thank you, Jesus for coming. Thank you for the hard seasons of waiting, the sweet seasons of celebration, and everything in between. This book is entirely yours. Bind my wandering heart to yours for all time, until I see you face to face.

Notes

1. Peterson, Eugene H. *The Jesus Way: A Conversation on the Ways That Jesus Is the Way*. Grand Rapids, MI: William B. Eerdmans Pub., 2007. Print.

2. Purifoy, Christie. *Roots & Sky A Journey Home In Four Seasons*. Grand Rapids, MI: Revell, 2016. Print.

3. L'Engle, Madeline. *Walking on Water*. Colorado Springs, CO: Waterbrook, 2001. Print.

4. Cairns, Scott, Greg Pennoyer, and Gregory Wolfe. *God with Us: Rediscovering the Meaning of Christmas*. Brewster Mass.: Paraclete, 2007. Print. (Cairns, 61)

5. http://articles.latimes.com/2014/mar/30/world/la-fg-wn-syria-journalists-freed-20140330

6. Tozer, A. W., and Samuel Marinus Zwemer. *The Pursuit of God*. Harrisburg, PA: Christian Publications, 1948. Print.

7. Miller, Paul E. *A Praying Life: Connecting with God in a Distracting World*. Colorado Springs, CO: NavPress, 2009. Print.

8. Cairns, Scott, Greg Pennoyer, and Gregory Wolfe. *God with*

Us: Rediscovering the Meaning of Christmas. Brewster Mass.: Paraclete, 2007. Print. (Norris, Kathleen 2007 101)

9-10. Bonhoeffer, Dietrich, and Jana Riess. *God Is in the Manger: Reflections on Advent and Christmas.* Louisville, KY: Westminster John Knox, 2010. Print.

11. Collier, Winn. *Restless Faith: Holding on to a God Just out of Reach.* Colorado Springs, CO: NavPress, 2005. Print.

12. "Come, Thou Fount of Every Blessing." *Come, Thou Fount of Every Blessing.* N.p., n.d. Web. 01 July 2016.

13. Miller, Paul E. *A Praying Life: Connecting with God in a Distracting World.* Colorado Springs, CO: NavPress, 2009. Print.

About The Author

As a sequin-wearing, homeschooling mother of four, Kris is passionate about Jesus, people and words. Her heart beats to share the hard, but glorious truth about life in Christ. She's been known to take gratuitous pictures of her culinary creations, causing mouths to water all across Instagram. Once upon a time, she ran 10 miles for **Compassion International,** a ministry for which she serves as an advocate. Kris is the author of, **Holey, Wholly, Holy: A Lenten Journey of Refinement,** and the follow up, **Companion Workbook.** In addition to contributing to multiple books, her writing has also been featured on numerous websites. She spends her free time managing GraceTable.org, organizing **Refine [the retreat]** and occasionally writing at **kriscamealy.com.**

Other Books

Finding Church: Stories of Finding, Switching, and Reforming (Civitas Press, 2012)

Holey, Wholly, Holy: A Lenten Journey Of refinement (Create Space 2013)

Holey Holey, Wholly: A Lenten Journey of Refinement, Companion Workbook (Create Space 2014)

Soul Bare: Stories of redemption (Contributor, IVP, 2016)

Craving Connection: 30 Challenges For real Life Engagement (Contributor, B&H Books, 2017)

The Heart of Marriage: Stories That Celebrate The Adventure Of Life Together (Contributor, Revell, 2017)

Made in the USA
Monee, IL
31 October 2019

16099690R00085